Stubborn Love

A Recommitment to Live When Giving
Up Seemed so Much Easier

Cheryl Ott

WestBow
PRESS
A DIVISION OF THOMAS NELSON

Unless otherwise noted all Scripture is from the New American Standard Version of the Bible.

AUTHORS NOTE: Some names have been changed to protect the privacy of individual's involved in some parts of this true-story.

WestBow Press books may be ordered through booksellers or by contacting:

WestBow Press
A Division of Thomas Nelson
1663 Liberty Drive
Bloomington, IN 47403
www.westbowpress.com
1-(866) 928-1240

Cover art by LoveArts Design Studios

ISBN: 978-1-4497-3358-2 (e)
ISBN: 978-1-4497-3359-9 (sc)
ISBN: 978-1-4497-3360-5 (hc)

Library of Congress Control Number: 2011961929

Printed in the United States of America

WestBow Press rev. date: 1/4/2012

"There are three ways of committing suicide:
taking my own life, letting myself die
and letting myself live without hope."
— Brennan Manning, author, Lion and Lamb

For those who have lost someone you love—to suicide.

Acknowledgments

My friend, Felicita Myers, your encouragement for me to submit my story for the writing contest was the push that I needed. Thank you. Women of Faith, Inc., your Writing Contest motivated me to finish a story I started writing seven years ago. Thank you.

Ever the cheerleader and friend, Christina May, you were the first to read chapter one, then two and finally the entire manuscript—out loud. You have served as a midwife to birth this baby. Thank you for your faithful and loving support.

God knew I would have lost my mind without you, Jackie Macgirvin, thank you for your skillful editorial assistance. When you said, "yes," to partner with God and me on this project, I knew everything was gonna be all right!

My faithful intercessors and friends, Ronnie Brown, Teresita Larentowicz, Marty Fulton, and Robyn & Martin Green I could not have endured this arduous process without your loving prayers and faithful support-- thank you.

My preview audience – my sisters – Christina Ortega, Shawna Summers, Darcy Weinhold, Jean Taylor, Betty Yater, Melanie Chiang, and my brotha, Jaret Wilson, thank you for your insightful feedback.

Thank you Robyn Green for your excellent freelance proofreading skills.

The book cover design is the work of Founder/Creative Director of LoveArts Design Studios, my brother, Joshua Dingle –thank you, bro. The author photo is the work of Kenneth Bentley @ LoveArts Photography –thank you, Kenny.

And last, but certainly not least, there may not have been a Cheryl Ott, author of Stubborn Love, without the skillful and necessary intervention of my best good friend, Theresa Noye. Friend, I'm so thankful that God allowed our paths to cross in the summer of 93'. I'll always be grateful that you allowed me the good fortune of being your first "white" friend. And how can I say, 'thanks' for listening to your gut and following the intervention protocol in March 96'. Quite possibly, I'm alive today because you cared, and by God's grace—intervened. Thank you, Friend.

Contents

Foreword

Cheryl is a beautiful woman, anointed, and on fire for God. She is passionate about helping the hurting. Her whole life is an offering poured out on the altar for the Lord and His people. Cheryl spends much of her time in worship and intercession doing the self-sacrificing work that many Christians neglect.

As her pastors of 10 years, we clearly see who she is now so when we read her journey of pain and victory we are reminded of the amazing transforming power of God to take our broken pieces and make a beautiful masterpiece of broken lives.

Just like the Lord brought Cheryl up from the grave of hopelessness, He can rescue anyone--from those struggling with depression and desperation—to those who are considering giving up on life.

You will be inspired by Cheryl's story. As you walk the journey with her you will hear the Lord whisper, "My love will never let you go."

Drs. Clarence and Ja'Ola Walker

The Walkers have appeared nationally on many radio and television programs including the 700 Club, and are featured speakers at conferences and seminars throughout the United States.

Pastors and Founders of *Fresh Anointing Christian Center*, Philadelphia.

Dr. Clarence Walker, author, *Biblical Counseling with African Americans* and *Breaking Strongholds in the African American Family.*

Dr. Ja'Ola Walker, author, *The 8 Powers of A Woman.*

Introduction

The American Foundation for Suicide Prevention estimates that every minute someone attempts suicide—approximately one million people every year. Every fifteen minutes someone dies by suicide, over 34,000 Americans each year.

Most people either know of someone or personally have lost a loved one to suicide. When a loved one dies by suicide a minimum of six other people have been catastrophically affected.

In 1999 the Surgeon General noted more teenagers and young adults die from suicide than from heart disease, cancer, birth defects, stroke, pneumonia, flu, chronic lung disease and AIDS—COMBINED.

Sadly, these numbers include Christians who did not have the coping skills needed to navigate through a crisis, depression or a temporary hardship. Instead, untreated depression, despair and hopelessness led to an acute depressive episode and they died by their own hand.

Tragically, suicide remains a topic largely ignored in the body of Christ, even though depression, despair and hopelessness are common responses to hardships, afflictions and crises for believers as well as non-believers.

Stubborn Love is a riveting story about a college student, in her twenties, and her fight to stay alive when giving up seemed so much easier. This is a true-story of her desperate struggle with acute depression, suicidal ideas and her suicide attempt.

This story is also about a dramatic rescue by Love. How He won the affection of her heart and rescued her from the black hole of suicidal despair. How He gave her hope and a future she never dreamed possible. I'm Cheryl and this is my story.

Part One

A Cry For Justice

Chapter 1

I'll Make Them Pay

"The pain of the mind is worse than the pain of the body."
Publilius Syrus (Roman author, first century BC)

I'll make them feel pain for their conditional love, I thought. *Wait. Was this my thought? Where did this idea come from?*

Yeah! That's what I'll do. I'll make them feel my pain forever. Suddenly, I realized I had a boisterous one hundred-voice choir in my head, echoing my thoughts and feelings.

Or was it their song reverberating in my head? *I don't know!* The disharmony of the voices never let up!

Go to the train tracks. Throw yourself in front of a fast train.

They won't know why I took my life. I have to write a letter, don't I? Yeah, I need to write a letter. I want them to know—they were responsible.

I grabbed my spiral notebook, ripped out a sheet, and began to scrawl my final goodbye.

Dear Family and Friends,

I am sorry to have caused you so much pain and embarrassment recently—so much that you wouldn't look me in the eyes during the entire weekend I was home for Christmas. Yes, I know it was because you couldn't bear the fact that I chose to cut my hair—a mortal sin according to your beliefs. Of course, you're also angry that I left the church, and I'm now going to a black church—even though they're also one God, apostolic, tongue talkers who are Jesus ONLY believers, as you would say. But, I don't get it! I don't understand how you could say that our church was the only way and had the truth, yet shun me. Where is the love? Or is only God's love unconditional? I can't bear the pain of conditional love. I knew what to expect when I chose to leave the church, cut my hair, pierce my ear lobes, and wear blue jeans. I've seen it my entire life. But, I was completely unprepared to experience the reality of conditional love for myself. The emotional pain and distance is simply too much. It haunts me day and night. It's all I think about. I needed your love. I'm sorry. I love you. By now, you may be feeling a measure of what I've been feeling for more than a year. Sorry, I just can't manage the torment and pain any longer.

Please forgive me.

Cheryl

Trembling inside and out, I folded the gloomy suicide note, tucked it inside an envelope, licked the flap, and sealed it.

I wrote the letter—done!

I opened my desk drawer and placed it inside.

Eventually, someone will find it, I guess.

The one hundred-voice choir chanted to me: *Go ahead. Kill yourself. Make them pay for their conditional love. Make them feel the pain you feel—FOREVER!*

Afraid that one of my friends would show up unannounced and intercept or delay my plans, I hurriedly put on my jean jacket, took a deep breath, glanced up and down the hall, and exited my dorm.

It was Saturday. Students were either in their rooms, the library, or off campus enjoying the day.

The field covered with fall foliage—once vibrant with hues of red, orange, and yellow had faded. The leaves crunched and crackled underfoot.

The scenic campus was no longer in view. The air was damp and chilly. I was cold and fear was building with each step.

My tight hamstring muscles were being stretched with every stride, up a very steep embankment. Out of breath, I reached the top of the rugged hill, looked down, and stared at the railroad tracks.

Any minute now, a train will speed by.

The dissonant choir in my head urgently chanted louder and LOUDER while my soul absorbed their message.

Just do it. Go ahead, just do it; they don't care anyway, no one cares.

Fearful, I kicked my feet across the dirt and noticed a corroded railroad spike. I held the cold metal in my hand and stared at the six-inch spike. *Does this look anything like the spikes that impaled Jesus' hands and feet? I don't even want to think about His suffering right now!*

Questions assaulted my mind.

I don't want to live with a disfigured face or a maimed body. What if I don't die? I don't want to fail. Can I do this? Is this really how I want my life to end?

The inharmonious choir with their jarring voices repeated the familiar stanza: *Go ahead. Kill yourself. Make them pay for their conditional love. Make them feel the pain you feel—FOREVER.* The tug of war continued between my ears.

Why do I need the unconditional love of my family and friends? Can't I learn to live without it?

I don't know. I'm so confused and depressed. Hot tears cascaded down my cold cheeks.

More afraid of the unknown than the known, I threw down the rusty spike and walked away from the tracks, down the embankment, and pensively strolled back to my cold, sterile dorm room.

My plan was derailed. *Now what?*

I jumped into my disheveled bed, pulled the goose down comforter over my head as I had nearly every day for the past several weeks, and prayed. *Please, God, please don't let me ever wake up.*

Twelve hours later, and much to my chagrin, I awoke.

I was overwhelmed. Panic engulfed me. I didn't have a plan B. *I'll probably fail all five classes. I've missed too many to catch up.*

The one hundred-voice choir had now grown to what sounds like two hundred assaulting voices.

Just do it. Go ahead. They don't care anyway. No one cares. The gloomy song continued.

Oh my God! I've got to get help. I'm too embarrassed to return to my classes. I don't want to hear my classmates say, "Oh, I thought you dropped," or, "where have you been?"

It's too complicated, my life! I don't want to face my professors either. Maybe I should go see that counselor my friend talked about, if I can even find her number.

I dialed three times. Each time, I hung up. *I don't know what to say. I'm too afraid.*

Hungry, I walked to the cafeteria for breakfast. My friend joined me.

"I'm not doing well, Friend. I can't seem to pull my life together."

"Did you call the counselor?"

"I tried, but I chickened out—didn't know what to say."

"Cheryl, please call her. Set an appointment—I really believe she can help."

"Really?"

"Yes!"

"Okay, I'll call her later today."

"I'll give you a ride if you need one."

"K. Thanks."

I walked back to my room.

My belly was filled with scrambled eggs, apple cinnamon pancakes, and hash browns. Food helped reduce my edginess.

Encouraged by my friend, I made the call. I had an appointment the next day.

The counselor began the session, "Cheryl, how can I help?"

"Uh, it's difficult to know where to begin. It's just that, uh, I don't know. I don't know where to begin."

"Tell me about yourself."

"Uh, myself, huh?"

She smiled and waited with a look of anticipation.

"Well, my friend told me that I should talk to you. I'm not doing very well."

"What's going on?"

"I'm failing all of my college classes."

"Failing?"

"I never go to class. I can't study. I can't think. I'm d ... de ... I'm depressed."

"About what, Cheryl?"

"Mostly my family and friends." Tears began to sneak out the corners of my eyes. She noticed and handed me a tissue.

"My entire world has shattered to millions of pieces, and I don't know what to do. I can't seem to function. Every day, it gets harder and harder for me just to get out of bed."

I felt comfortable telling this complete stranger my story. She listened well and asked thought-provoking questions. I must have rambled on for twenty minutes.

I began to see her twice a week.

She introduced me to a psychiatrist who prescribed anti-depressant medication for what he described as a major depressive disorder.

My counselor seemed to care a lot. But, it felt like we talked about the same thing—I relive and repeat the same stories of injustice.

"Cheryl, you will eventually learn to live without your family and friends' unconditional love."

"But, it hurts so bad!"

"The pain will ease with time; you'll develop a new set of expectations and relational skills for dealing with your family and friends."

"But, I want justice right now! I want to hear them say, 'I'm sorry, Cheryl, for causing you pain. Please, forgive me.'"

Will I ever hear those words, and if so, how many months or years must I wait? Can I wait? And, what do I do with this gnawing, internal pain?

I gritted my teeth and tried to stuff it.

I tried to shelf it.

I tried to compartmentalize it.

But, the pain is stored in the strained muscle fibers of my neck. I can't turn my head—my neck is locked.

Ouch. These disabling, acute muscle spasms—this is a real pain in the neck.

I can't sleep. Pressure. Pressure. *So much pressure!*

This reminds me of those days when Mom and Grammy would spend hours in a hot summer kitchen canning garden produce. They used an old, stainless steel pressure cooker that had a noisy jigger valve—a pressure regulator that rocked back and forth on top of the lid. It sounded like the cooker would explode if the pressure continued.

Well, my emotional jigger valve was going crazy, and I didn't know how to release the pressure inside.

Chapter 2

Snowball Effect

"A human being is a deciding being."
—Viktor Frankl

I received a call from my ex-boyfriend, affectionately called Curious George. It was one month before his wedding day, and he called just to say, "Cheryl, I will *ALWAYS* love you, but, my commitment to Sara overrides my feelings for you."

You see, George and I decided a couple years earlier, that our relationship was too complicated. In spite of our deep love for each other, neither of us had the courage to weather the turbulence of an interracial relationship (he's black, I'm white).

According to our church's beliefs, it was against God's command to marry outside of your race. No one was going to support our relationship. Not my parents. Not my church friends. Not the college administration. No one!

Our secret relationship went on for nearly three years. Our song was Dolly Parton's "I Will Always Love You." So, when George said, "I will *ALWAYS* love you," he was referring to our song.

Two years passed by after our relationship ended, and George and I communicated less and less. Now, George was getting married. I was so confused. Since when does "commitment override feelings of love"? I guess I'm supposed to be flattered by that statement. In some strange way I was.

Days later, I'd received a call from my current boyfriend, Evan, who lived out-of-state.

Years earlier when George and I concluded that we'd no longer continue our relationship, he made me promise him that I'd never marry any other black guy. If he—a black man—couldn't marry me, then he wanted no other black man to marry me. His request made perfect sense to me. After all, the only reason we weren't going to be together was because his skin was black and mine white.

Evan was our mutual college friend, and he met the racial criteria. He was extremely handsome, fun, and incredibly passionate about his faith.

Evan was a senior in high-school when he received Christ into his heart. During the course of his senior year, Evan persuaded more than eighty non-believing classmates to accept Christ. He was quite the evangelist.

George believed that Evan would be a perfect match for me. I trusted George, and felt that if I couldn't marry him, then Evan would be the next best choice.

We'd been dating for six months when he called.

"Hi, Evan."

"Hi Cheryl, guess what?"

"You're coming to see me?" I responded wistfully.

"No, I'm going to be a daddy!"

"A what? What are you talking about?"

"You see. Well, I had this one night with my high-school sweetheart, and well, she found out that she's going to be the Mother of my child. She's pregnant!"

"And, I'm supposed to be excited for you?" Confused, I hung up the phone. I knew that my relationship with Evan was over.

By this point, I was devastated. I felt like I'd lost everyone. And now I didn't have love—not the love of my family or my church friends. Not the love of George, not really, nor Evan's love. *Oh God! This magnetic black hole of despair and hopelessness is sucking me in.*

I was so angry.

I was angry with friends.

I was angry at how the church ostracized me.

I was angry that I couldn't get over their conditional love.

I was angry with George for stringing my heart along, and setting me up with Evan.

I was angry with Evan for not being faithful.

I was angry with myself for caring about anyone.

I was sooooo angry!

Days later, Mom called out of the blue.

"Listen Cheryl, I thought you'd want to know the doctors have given uncle Steven only two weeks to live."

"What? Two weeks? Why?"

"Well, they found out he has a terminal disease and they won't be able to operate. If you want to see him you should do it this week."

I hung up the phone and cried, and cried some more.

My entire world shattered to pieces all around me.

Why is there so much pain? I can't do this! I don't want to live my life in this much pain.

This was my favorite uncle, my uncle Steven.

I immediately went to visit him in the hospital. This too was unbearable.

"Uncle Steven, I'll always cherish the red leather bound, Thompson Chain Reference Bible you gave me for Christmas, when I was fifteen."

He didn't respond.

"You've always been my favorite uncle. You're very special to me."

"No, I'm not special, Cheryl."

His response broke my heart.

"Yes, you are! You are special! You're special to me."

Why didn't he feel special?

His statement haunted me.

I didn't like the way death swallowed him suddenly, two weeks later.

A week after we laid my favorite uncle to rest, I was distraught. I was failing my classes again. I'd suffered so much loss in such a short period of time. I didn't have the coping skills to overcome the immense pain that had a stranglehold on my heart.

The two hundred-voice choir, continued to sing the same ole song, I'd been forced to endure for more than six months.

"Go ahead. Kill yourself. Make them pay for their conditional love. Make them feel the pain you feel—FOREVER."

It seemed like it never stopped.

I felt my life spin out of control.

My counselor thought maybe I may be Bipolar, or Manic-depressive.

I didn't care about a diagnosis.

I hurt really badly inside.

I didn't know what that made me except one badly hurting young woman.

I felt like my little boat was officially capsized in this turbulent ocean called life. It had become very apparent I'd never learned how to swim in anything deeper than a lil' kiddy wading pool. I didn't have the skills to navigate this stormy ocean. I didn't know what to do when tsunami-like waves pummeled me.

I just knew I couldn't breathe.

I couldn't swim.

I didn't have an ounce of strength to keep my head above water. What was I supposed to do?

Frustrated, confused, angry, and desperate I reached inside my kitchen cabinet, pulled out a short cobalt blue drinking glass, and hurled it to the floor.

I liked the way that felt.

It shattered into a million different sized pieces.

I liked the sound of shattered glass.

Because it was something I could control?

Because that sound represented what happened to my fragile heart? I didn't know.

I reached for another. It made a louder sound this time as shattered blue glass smacked shattered blue glass.

The cacophony of voices chanted, *"Just do it. Go ahead. They don't care anyway; no one cares. Go ahead and kill yourself."*

I fell to the kitchen floor, and sat right in the middle of all the blue pieces.

I picked up a glass shard shaped like an arrowhead.

I stared.

The blue glass talked to me.

"Carve into your arm with me."

The choir chanted, "Forgotten."

I carved '4gotten' into my right arm.

A time to die, the choir chanted.

I obediently carved, 'A Time 2 DIE' into my left arm.

I'd never thought about cutting before.

Who does this? Where did this idea come from? Maybe, I am Manic, or Bipolar, or whatever. Wow. That didn't even hurt. It actually felt kind of good.

The emotional pain was so excruciating that when I'd cut myself, it just didn't hurt—it seemed to take the focus off of the emotional pain I felt. The emotional pain was much greater than the physical pain.

"Do it again," the choir chanted.

"Trash," whispered a solo voice.

Following the instruction, I carved 'TRASH' into both of my legs. *At least, when they find me, they'll have some insight into how I felt about my life.*

My insides screamed, "Justice, I want justice!"

But there was no justice in any of this.

There was no justice in my experiences.

I wanted wrong things in my life to be made right.

Would they ever be?

How could they?

I'd never have George's love or Evan's.

I'd never have my family or friends unconditional love.

I'd never see my favorite uncle Steven again.

There was no justice anywhere.

I took matters into my own hands.

Blood streamed from my arms and legs.

What's happening to me?

The two hundred-voice choir became a five hundred-voice choir.

The dissonance of the voices made me reel.

Someone make the voices stop, please, make'em stop. Can anybody hear me? Help me?

I couldn't breathe.

I couldn't think.

I needed oxygen.

The black hole was sucking me in.

I had no strength—emotional, or physical.

I couldn't resist its strong magnetic pull.

I'd lost my grip.

This was a time to die.

Chapter 3

Emergency Rescue

"If you will send for a doctor, I will see him now."
—Emily Jane Brontë

The next morning in the ER:

"Cheryl, do you want to die?" the resident hospital psychiatrist asked smugly.

I avoided his eyes.

"Ummm. No. Not really!" I shrugged.

"Can you tell me why you carved into your arms?"

"Sure," I said sarcastically, "because, it's my body, and I can do whatever I want to it!"

"Cheryl, when you carve into your arms it's called self-injury"

"Well, it's my body and my art—its body-art!"

"Cheryl, it's called self-mutilation and I could have you committed for this," he scolded.

"Well, it's no different than the tattoo on your arm!" I boldly declared. "You just spent $200 for yours and I did mine for free!"

"Cheryl," he continued, "Here are your choices. You can voluntarily check yourself into this psych ward for seven days, or I will have you involuntarily committed to the State Hospital."

He handed me the clipboard to involuntarily/voluntarily sign myself in. I'd heard horror stories about state hospitals.

"That's hardly a choice doctor! That's an ultimatum!"

"I'm glad you learned that four-syllable word, Cheryl. Now what will it be?"

I detected sarcasm.

I snatched the clipboard and scribbled my signature dramatically on the intake form.

"A nurse will be with you shortly," he said as he left the room.

The clock on the wall went out of focus as tears flooded my eyes. The night before, I'd cut myself to anesthetize the pain of my heart. In the ER, I sobbed until I was completely in touch with the reality of my situation. My heart was anything but numb—I was in so much pain.

How am I ever going to make it through this?

The nurse escorted me to the hospital's psych ward and to a tiny, cold, sterile room.

"I need your shoelaces and belt. It's for your own safety. You're on suicide watch for the next 48 hours."

I'd never thought about using shoelaces or a belt. Ouch, who would choose that method?

The nurse left the room. I laid down on my bed in complete disbelief.

How did I end up here? This wasn't on my agenda.

Fifteen minutes later the nurse returned. I was annoyed when I learned she would check on me to make sure I was still alive. I was irritated as her flashlight woke me every fifteen minutes.

I was able to make one phone call, so I called my psychotherapist.

"Hi, Susan, umm, could you make a phone call to the hospital psychiatrist and get me outta here?"

"No, Cheryl. I won't be able to do that. The best advice I can give you is to follow instructions, and get the help you need so that you can be released in seven days."

Disappointed, I hung up and hunkered down.

Face it—this will be your reality for the next seven days.

With nothing to do I walked to the common area—the psych lounge. Some talked to the TV. Some talked to themselves, or their imaginary friends.

These people are really crazy out here.

One older woman resisted the nurse; she refused to take her medication. They bantered back and forth. The woman became enraged and spouted off delusional threats. Husky men dressed in all white rushed in and administered a tranquilizer to the woman's arm. She was put in restraints and carried away.

"They're takin' her to the dark, solitary room," smirked a disheveled woman.

I gotta get out of here. Everyone's so scary! Can't cause any trouble; don't want anyone giving me a shot and sending me to the dark, solitary room.

I quickly made up my mind that whatever I needed to do and say to these people, I would.

What did they want to hear? What would earn me a day-pass?

My new goal was to be honorably discharged from this hospital psych ward at the end of seven days.

My pastor found out that I was in the psych ward and he did what any good pastor would do—he came to visit.

"Cheryl, do you know why you're here? Do you see all of those people over there?"

"Yes."

"Well what do you see?"

"I see a lot of crazy folk, yeah, there's a lot of crazy people here!"

"Yes, and you're here for them!"

"Huh?"

"Cheryl, you're ministry material."

"Ministry material? Uh, excuse me Bishop, Dr., Rev., Pastor, but I spent three years, and a lot of money in a Bible college, to earn the title 'ministry material,' and that didn't work out so well. Now, I'm 302'd and this suddenly qualifies me as 'ministry material?'"

"That's right, Cheryl. You got it! Now, I want you to stop running from God's call on your life and the work of the ministry, and I want you to start attending our Minister training classes regularly! You're a Minister," he declared. "I'll see you next Sunday, Cheryl." He grabbed his winter coat and hat, and turned to leave.

I felt a little more hopeful, so I attended the psych ward's group therapy.

I went to art and music therapy.

I took my prescribed meds without resistance.

I met with the hospital psychiatrist for daily evaluations.

All of this earned me a day-pass, which meant that I could spend several hours one evening with church friends.

I went to *family night* at their house. Everyone in the family was at the table. I was choking on my embarrassment. Everyone knew that I'd attempted suicide, and was presently 302'd, and out on a "good behavior" pass.

My friends seemed afraid to make eye contact and didn't know what to say.

I wanted to run, but had no place to go. And if I bolted, it would earn me an extended stay in the psych ward. I sure didn't want that. I clenched my teeth and pretended that I was okay.

I focused on enjoying the succulent dinner—fried and baked chicken, bbq ribs, and roast beef so tender it melted in my mouth. Mmmm. Real potatoes—roasted and mashed—with butter, sour cream and garlic. And the buttery, hot cheese dinner rolls where simply otherworldly.

For a very brief moment, I felt like I'd died and gone to Heaven. I was sure I was eating Heaven's food until someone asked, "Are you out of the hospital or do you have to go back tonight?"

All five of the separate table conversations, none of which I was part of, ceased, and everyone stretched their necks like paparazzi journalists to hear my response.

"Uh," I stuttered. "Yes, I do have to return to the hospital tonight for a couple more days."

"Oh," they said in unison, and resumed their conversations.

I was mortified! I felt like I had leprosy or some other contagious disease.

Are people afraid they might say the one thing that would set me off and cause me to attempt suicide? Do they think I'm insane—a crazy person? Do they think I'm so fragile that they can't have an honest conversation about why I attempted suicide? Are they completely clueless, and simply don't know what to say—or, one of my favorite multiple-choice responses, all of the above?

I returned to the hospital that night.

Two days later, I was officially released from the hospital psych ward.

Chapter 4

The Stigma

"I see people, as they approach me, trying to make up
their minds whether they'll 'say something about it' or
not. I hate if they do, and if they don't."
—C.S. Lewis

I returned to my college campus, and felt like I had the mark of
the beast tattooed on my forehead. People stared at me, and then
around me, as if they didn't see me. I was too embarrassed to go to
my classes, to face the students and my instructors.

Everyone thinks I'm crazy!

Not one student ever had the courage to question me. None
of my instructors engaged me in conversation about the incident,
homework, yes, but not my suicide attempt.

To be honest, I didn't want to talk about it. I wanted the entire
episode to be quickly forgotten.

Suicide must rank as one of the top three subjects we never talk
about. There is such a stigma around this issue. Why? Maybe its
because it's an "*S*" word.

While growing up, I was never allowed to say certain "*S*" words
like "*Shut-up*" or "*Stupid*" or even "*Shoot*" (another word for a
certain four letter expletive). The word "*Sex*" was never spoken in

my home, nor was it ever a subject of conversation—not even in generalities. *Suicide* was not a topic of discussion either.

I remember having dinner with my family one evening, and we received a dreadful phone call that our friend's father had shot and killed himself that morning at his home.

I remember seeing Dad's compassionate face turn white as a sheet. And Mom was horrified.

"Why would he *do that* to himself? How could he *do that* to his family?" she asked my daddy rhetorically.

"Do what?" we asked.

Our friend's were quick to make sense of why their father had taken such extreme measures to end his pain.

1) He was physically in a tremendous amount of pain and he simply couldn't manage it any longer.

2) Nothing seemed to comfort or ease his pain; it was becoming more intense day by day.

3) The doctors could not help him; medications did not help him.

4) The agonizing physical pain left him psychologically vulnerable.

5) In his mind, the pain would never end, so he took matters into his own hand, and ended his pain—which ended his life.

This was clearly a cry for justice—for wrong things in his life to be made right—namely the pain in his physical body to end.

I remember the stigma and sensitivity around his death. Appropriately, everyone wanted to safeguard the image and honor of this man; everyone wanted to protect the immediate family. In their minds, the best thing to do was to *never* talk about the incident that ended their loved one's life. And no one ever said he "*died by suicide.*"

I was thirteen when I watched a murder/suicide TV mystery late one night. I was shocked when I learned that young people attempted suicide and some succeeded.

Why? What could be so terrible about a teenager's life that they would want to end their life by suicide?

I didn't get it.

I was upset.

In that moment, I felt like an arrow from Heaven pierced my heart, and I heard the voice of God inside me say, "Cheryl, one day I want you to bring a message of hope to these hurting and hopeless ones."

I went into the bathroom, buried my face in my hands, and sobbed uncontrollably. From that moment my heart was marked.

I never told anyone about the TV show, or subsequent conversation with God about bringing a message of hope to those so desperate they wanted to end their lives. I just understood that I should *never* talk about it because I was *never* to talk about *Suicide*.

Chapter 5
Bonjour Paris

"O God, I have tasted Thy goodness, and it has both satisfied me and made me thirsty for more... give me grace to rise and follow Thee up from this misty lowland where I have wandered so long."
—A.W. Tozer

I continued to see my psychotherapist, Susan. I learned coping and relational skills to help me overcome the pain of conditional love, and the strained relationship with my family and friends.

As my pastor required, I attended the next 52 weeks of *Ministers Training* class. The only thing I'd learned was that I had a lot more responsibilities to *do*.

I was required to attend two Sunday services, Wednesday night Bible study, and Friday evening service. I was also on the worship team, which required a separate rehearsal time and prayer meeting. I was appointed the Assistant Director of the youth ministry, which necessitated separate meetings and scheduled events. I was so exhausted from *doing, doing,* and *doing.* I just needed to *be.*

My girlfriend, Mel, a beloved friend from Bible college, came to visit me to explore how she felt about moving from Canada to Philadelphia to get a job and possibly continue her education.

A few weeks after her visit, Mel called, "Cheryl, I've been looking into nanny jobs in Paris. Why don't we do it together? Why don't we go to Paris and become Au Pairs? How about it?"

I discussed the audacious idea on the phone with her.

"Sure, why not? I could earn twelve language credits, and it would qualify as a study abroad program too."

Within a few weeks, I bravely purchased my airline ticket to Paris, France!

We arrived in Paris in late August. Paris—the city of Lights—a city filled with culture, fashion, arts and romance. The only French word I knew was "bonjour". Admittedly, that was a good place to start.

The Walsh's, the family I would work for, met me at the Charles de Gaulle Airport.

Mel and I parted ways. She'd work for a family thirty minutes away. I was on my own.

The Walsh's drove me to my new Parisian residence, showed me to my petite bedroom, and then called me to the dinner table. Can you say, "culture shock"?

Before we ate, I was introduced to the two younger children, Marion, 8, and David, 10. They had two older brothers 15 and 18. The older boys certainly didn't need an Au Pair, but I needed them—they spoke English.

David was just beginning to learn English, and Marion had not begun to learn English, yet. Bernard and Isabelle, the Dad and Mom, both spoke English. I was relieved because I couldn't speak French at all!

The family sat at the table to eat. *Ah, the delectable smell of French cuisine.*

I sat in an upholstered European chair, at the round pedestal dining table, and noticed my dinner plate had a dead fish with its body wrapped in aluminum foil. What's worse, the slimy, scaly fish was looking right at me!

Why? I didn't bait and catch him, or remove him from his watery world. But, he wouldn't take his eye off me. Inside, I was freaking out. *This was a horrible practical joke to play on the Au Pair.*

Then, I noticed that everyone had a fish head and body wrapped in aluminum foil.

Where am I? I have never eaten a fish in my life. I grew up on Gorton's breaded fish sticks, fish filets, and Star-Kist white chunk tuna in a can. But I've never eaten a real fish before!

Frankly, I didn't like the idea of beginning now.

I didn't even know how to eat *Nemo*.

So, I quietly observed.

They unwrapped the fish, tossed the foil, and slowly pulled the meat off the bones. I'd heard the French had a passionate love affair with food, but this was *over the top*.

The fact that it was Salmon made no difference to me. I didn't want to eat the fish. Nor did I want to be rude or offensive. I had just arrived fifteen minutes earlier.

They served me couscous pilaf, another dish I had never eaten before. It was made with carrots, almonds, and chickpeas. I used this tasty pilaf to mask the taste of salmon.

As I was eating, I chomped on a tiny little fish bone. It stabbed me in the back of my throat.

Cough, cough.

"Are you okay Chérie?

Cough.

"Yeah. Something just got me in the back of my throat."

Just about chocked to death. Cough. Darn bones!

"I'm fine. Thanks."

I left a whole lot of meat on that salmon's bones. I wasn't about to experience the Heimlich maneuver on my first day in Paris.

I was worn out after two days of travel. So, I excused myself and told the family I'd probably sleep through the evening, and see them the next morning.

Once alone in my au pair sleeping quarters, I locked my door and cried.

I felt like Jonah, who'd run away from God, and ended up in a foreign place—the belly of a great fish. Well, you know how I feel about fish? This was foreign to me—everything was foreign to me.

We'd driven from the airport on the opposite side of the road. The driver drove from the passenger side of the car. And, we had to drive on circles, called roundabouts, to make our highway exits. This was completely foreign to me.

I didn't know the language or the culture. I was completely overwhelmed and I sobbed all night.

"God, I'm so sorry, that like Jonah, I've run away from ministry and the call You have on my life. I've sinned and tried to escape. Please forgive me; I repent. In the morning, I'll have Bernard take me back to the airport and I'll go home."

As I cried and prayed, the Lord gave me Proverbs 19:21: "Many are the plans in a man's heart, but the counsel of the LORD will stand."

God assured me that He had a plan, too, and I did *not* need to go home. I needed to settle in.

I picked up my disc-man and played Kent Henry's *Jeremiah 29:11* CD.

It comforted me.

Finally, I drifted off to sleep.

I awoke the next morning with courage, and confidence that God had a great plan for this season of my life.

I was off to the American Consulate to register as an American citizen. Next, I registered for classes at the University of Sorbonne to study the French language and culture.

Soon I began to settle into my role as an Au Pair.

I worked from 3pm—9pm, five days a week.

My responsibilities: to do laundry, meet Marion at her school at 3pm, and the thorn in my side—prepare dinner for the family.

I was terrified to cook.

My fears were quickly confirmed.

The family did not enjoy my American culinary skills, the meals contained too much fat, and they discussed this amongst themselves over dinner—in *French*! They'd often laugh in my face.

Each afternoon David would walk through the door after school, go directly to the stove, and lift the lids off of pots to see and smell what he'd be eating for dinner.

One night, I was so excited to offer them a comforting winter treat—carrot soup. I'd enjoyed eating it in a Philadelphia café. In my opinion, it was simply delightful.

This particular afternoon, David came in and noticed a large pot on the stove.

"What's for dinner, Chérie?" he asked with a big smile.

"It's carrot soup, David!"

"What's carrot soup?" he inquired with his wrinkled nose and furrowed brow.

"Simply carrots pureed with seasoning and topped with a swirl of sour cream from the center to the rim. I really enjoy it."

I watched the horror and disappointment appear in David's eyes. Within a few minutes David told Marion.

They collaborated, called their Mom, and pleaded with her to order them pizza. She had pity and gave them their hearts desire. I was mortified.

Not one person in the entire family took a bite of that delicious soup I'd slaved over for hours.

Thank God it was Friday and I could disappear for the weekend. Hopefully that'd be enough time to build up my courage to go back into the kitchen on Monday.

I hated doing the laundry.

Everything was smaller in Paris: cars, houses, portions of food, and the washing machine. It was half the size of an American washer, and I washed *fourteen loads* every week! And they didn't have a dryer. Instead, I hung the wash in the musty basement and many times I had to iron the clothes.

Not my idea of *fun*!

I went to school every day to study Français; I started in the Beginner's class. This seemed appropriate for someone who only knew *"bonjour"*.

The instructor only spoke French in class—*intimidating*!

The class was full of students from many different countries.

I loved the diversity.

My instructor was trying to get a sense of who was in her class, and invited students to come to the chalkboard, and draw their nation's flag. I wasn't the only American in the class, but worked up enough courage to represent the USA.

This was completely uncharacteristic of me.

I never raised my hand.

To have the entire class turn to look at me was nerve-racking.

I lacked confidence in those situations.

And why I raised my hand on that day, I'll never know. I guess I was trying to embrace this new season, this new foreign experience.

With this newfound sense of courage, I marched up to the chalkboard, picked up the chalk, and proceeded to draw a picture of my nation's flag. I was confident in the stars and stripes design. But, in that awkward moment, I'd completely forgotten if the color behind the stars of my esteemed country's flag was red or blue?

Low-level chuckles came from various parts of the classroom behind me.

I was humiliated.

"Fait quelqu'un veut aider?" The instructor asked.

Look where my newfound courage had gotten me.

I was embarrassed. I felt like I'd somehow failed my country, and perpetuated the "stupid American" stereotype.

I'll have to endure that humiliation for the next few months.

Three months after I arrived in Paris, I returned home for a wedding. I promised my younger sister that I'd be her Maid of Honor.

I arrived in Philadelphia, and assumed the Maid of Honor role. My sister was stressed to the point of tears. My job was to support her and make sure her wedding day was everything she desired. The wedding itself was lovely, but I was thrilled when the reception was over. It's a lot of work to be the Maid of Honor on jet lag!

After the reception, I returned to my parents home to gather my things and say goodbye. I had to catch a flight the next morning to Paris.

Mom and Dad were happy the wedding was over, and they decided to continue the celebration by going out to a restaurant—alone. Dad was going to enjoy every minute of his black and white tuxedo! And Mom was beautiful in her wedding attire, a jade green formal length skirt suit.

It was time to say goodbye. I hugged Mom, then Dad. A thought flashed through my mind while we embraced.

What if this was the last time I would ever hug or see my daddy? Would something happen to him or would something happen to me? Would I be in Paris longer than a year? Would I follow God to Africa?

I didn't know—I still remember the embrace like it was yesterday. The next day I was back in Paris.

I met my friend Mel on Saturdays and Sundays. We'd visit the typical tourist attractions, eat brunch at a French café on the famous Champs-Élysées, and visit a bookstore or museum.

We were always on an adventure.

A couple of months passed, and we both longed to find a church where we could worship, and maybe meet new friends. Eventually, we found one—Hope International. I think I was particularly drawn to the church simply because of its name—*Hope*. We visited a couple of times and enjoyed the services. It was so much fun to meet new friends both Parisian and internationals.

The church had a library, which really didn't interest me, but one book caught my eye: *Whatever Happened To Worship*, by A.W. Tozer.

I'd asked God this question for nearly five years. Curious to see if the author could really answer my question, I returned to my au pair quarters and to my surprise, I literally devoured the book.

The author's words pierced my heart so deeply, so profoundly that I wept. I took copious notes on nearly every page. I was awed by the presence of God I encountered as I read.

It provoked me to go on a quest to experience God's presence for myself. A groan for nearness to God's heart stirred within. I spent hours, night after night, and sacrificed sleep to experience His presence—His heart.

I was soon addicted to A.W. Tozer's writings. I read every book I could get my hands on. I had legal pads full of notes. But, my heart, oh my heart, it burned again for the pursuit of God. I longed for His presence. I longed to feel His nearness. My appetite for His presence grew; my heart was tenderized so much that I wept when I read the Bible.

I read and studied the writings of A.W. Tozer more than I studied the French language or culture. I wanted to have a life in God like he did and I'd spend as much time as it took in order to have it!

In my teenage years, I'd experienced God's presence. I craved nearness to His heart. My heart was filled with striving to be good enough to experience His closeness.

Suddenly, I began to see God from another perspective. My heart and life in God became explosive. I felt like I could walk on air.

My heart soared again!

It'd been *sooo* long since I'd experienced God's nearness or presence. Not because He wasn't close, but because I'd grown weary with church. I'd grown weary of the weekly theatrics that characterized my experience with church. I wanted God, but I didn't want to *do church*.

I was taught that if you wanted God, you had to go to church, and since I was weary of church, I didn't pursue God for that season.

I simply existed.

I ached for God, but did not search for Him.

I soon became fascinated with my secret life in God. I experienced His closeness, and the weight of His presence in my au pair quarters, night after night, month after month. It felt like a honeymoon with God.

This was one of the best seasons of my entire life.

I had His heart and He had all of mine.

For the first time, I realized I no longer needed my family and friends approval or acceptance on every area of my life. I needed God's approval, and I had it every day and every night. He drew me closer and closer.

Things I'd thought I could never live without simply lost their pull; the power of His love changed my heart.

My chemistry literally began to change.

I felt alive, happy and full of light in my inner man.

I was grateful and completely enthralled with God.

I began to pray, "God, wherever You want me to go, I'll go."

I'd prayed this prayer a time or two during my teenage years, but it was so long since I'd really meant it. I was undone! His love had wrecked my heart. He'd won the affections of my whole heart!

"God, even if You want me to go to some remote place like Africa, I will go. I'll go and tell them what You're really like."

By this point, I joined the church worship team.

Yes, I signed up for God and the church all over again.

I couldn't get enough of His presence.

I told God I'd leave everything behind if I could just live close to His heart. And I meant it!

Sure, I loved my family, but I loved Him more. I didn't want to ever live without His nearness again. I loved the tingling, warm feelings my heart experienced. I loved my spirit-man living vibrantly and fully alive in God. I loved feeling my heart expand inside, bursting with new capacity for God. I didn't want to live without it, I simply couldn't.

I studied enough French to pass the class. I lived and worked as an Au Pair, I taught ESL (English as a second language) to a Korean businessman, immersed myself in the French culture, and explored Paris week after week.

Life was great, but none of these things caused my heart to soar. I wanted to feel God's presence, His nearness more.

Christmas in Paris

I loved Christmas.

This would be my very first Christmas away from my family. Since I'd been home in late November, I couldn't afford to return for the holidays. I felt the ache of not being with my family.

Mom had just returned home on Christmas Day after a two-week tour of Israel. Dad missed her so much. He'd never flown and vowed that he never would. I think he was afraid something would happen to Mom while she was away; she returned home safely on Christmas.

But, I wasn't there.

And I missed them, so I called. I spoke to Daddy last. With tears in his voice he said, "Baby, there's no place like home for the holidays."

Pushing back tears, I responded, "Yeah Daddy, you're right." We hung up. It was a sad, lonely day. But, I told myself—*it's Christmas in Paris. This may be a once-in-a-lifetime opportunity. So, try to make the most of it.*

Mel wasn't available on Christmas. Her French family enjoyed spectacular Christmas festivities. Mine did not. So, I spent Christmas alone on the Champs Élysées, one of the most famous streets in the world. It had lots of specialty shops, charming restaurants and cafés, book and music stores, and cinémas. It was hard to stay sad in Paris. The city was magnificent and glorious in beauty.

The next day, Mel and I would leave Paris for a multi-country road trip.

The Day After Christmas in London

Mel and I began our road trip. We were thrilled.

First, we had to get across the *English Channel*. We took the fastest and cheapest way to go from Paris to London. *Eurostar,* a high-speed passenger train, took us through a tunnel undersea to London's *Waterloo Station* at 186 mph.

We picked up our car rental, and joked about being *Thelma and Louise.*

The one square mile city of London is bananas to drive in.

It's a circus, for real. I'm not talking about *Piccadilly Circus.* Someone should've warned us *not* to attempt driving in downtown London.

The rental car was tiny with no front or rear bumpers.

Mel was great with maps and I was not. So, I opted to drive first.

The traffic was chaotic.

I should've looked at a London road rules manual.

Neither of us had ever driven on the opposite side of the highway, and we had *never* driven from the passenger side of the car. Let alone, shifting the standard with our left hand, at the same time.

Everything was backwards.

We knew nothing about roundabouts, a circular intersection, with multiple exits from which you must jump off.

It was a new driving experience.

It was nerve-wrecking.

Staying calm was the name of the game.

Getting out of London was insanity.

Once on the open roads, I decided to stay in the slow lane until I was more comfortable navigating the highway. Seemed like a smart thing to do.

I felt I was doing a pretty good job staying calm in these backward circumstances, until I saw flashing lights in my rearview mirror.

I had no idea what I'd done. I was in the slow lane and I'd driven with caution.

I gave the officer my International Driver's License. He informed me that I was driving too slow in the fast lane.

"This isn't America, lady. Welcome to England where we do things the proper way."

I promised to move to the slow lane; the far left-hand side of the highway.

I was so glad when we'd found our Bed & Breakfast accommodations. I could get off those crazy roads.

It was our first night in London.

The next day we would sightsee.

The people's Princess, Diana, had tragically died only four months earlier. People from all over the world still visited Windsor Castle to pay their respects, and were still mourning.

We visited the Tower of London, Westminster Abbey, and attended a service at St. Paul's Cathedral. We saw Tower Bridge and Big Ben.

It was a great day.

The following day, we drove several hours to Sheffield, England, known as "the largest village in England," to stay with a friend for a couple of days.

New Year's In Edinburgh, Scotland

We were back on the road, *Thelma and Louise*, driving to Scotland.
This was such a wonderful adventure.
We were having a blast!
The city was quite charming and romantic. We strolled through the streets, enjoyed Edinburgh's timeless elegance and fascinating history.
It was New Year's Eve in Edinburgh!
The New Year's celebration is very much a Scottish tradition that has migrated around the world. There were bagpipes and typical Scottish attire.
Expectation whipped through the crowd, and when the countdown hit midnight everyone erupted into hugging, kissing, singing and dancing. It was wonderful to experience part of my ancestral roots.
The next morning, we returned to Paris to resume our respective Au Pair roles.
One Saturday in March I called home. Mom was the only one home so we enjoyed a long conversation. I simply enjoyed listening to her voice. She shared her heart with me about her decision to leave her interior design job, and her desire to care for the sick and shut-in.
Mom went on to tell me that my uncle Walter, daddy's older brother, was in the hospital, and the doctors had given him only two months to live. I was sad to hear the news and even more sad for my daddy's heart. I told Mom that if this happened, I wouldn't have the financial resources to return for his funeral. She understood and our bittersweet conversation ended.

Chapter 6

The Best And Worst Day Of My Life

"It was the best of times. It was the worst of times."
—Charles Dickens

It was a lovely Saturday in Paris. I was invited to tour a French *Château*, a magnificent ancient castle of the Renaissance period with Mr. Baek (my ESL student) and his wife. It was such a treat to experience the grandeur and rich history of this castle; the beautiful gardens stood in contrast to its defense and fortification capabilities. It was breathtaking.

Over a three-course lunch at a *brasserie*, Mr. Baek put his conversational English to practice.

After lunch, we parted ways and I took the train to meet the worship team I was part of at my new church.

My heart soared.

I loved this season of my life.

I loved feeling the presence of God.

I was excited to go to rehearsal; I arrived 45 minutes early.

No one was around.

No problem. I'll just spend some time singing to God.

I began to sing songs to the Lord. This was one of the best 45-minute worship experiences of my life. My heart was burning with love for God.

The worship team arrived and we rehearsed for our Sunday morning service.

I had to return home pretty quickly because Bernard and Isabelle had a *date* night and I had to stay home with David and Marion.

David and Marion were such a delight. I genuinely enjoyed them. Marion was really into the *Spice Girls*, an English pop girls group. In fact, her father had just purchased tickets to see them in concert in Paris; Marion was really excited. She wanted to learn all their songs so she'd be able to sing along at the concert.

Marion was only beginning to learn English, so it was a challenge for her. But, she was determined to learn every English lyric of the *Spice Girls* songs.

David, Marion, and I played games late into the night, way past their bedtime. Finally, they went to bed.

I went to my room to be with God.

The day was fantastic and full. I was wonderfully tired. I had to get up pretty early the next morning to make it to church on time, so I decided to go to bed early, 1:00 a.m. With music in my ears, I fell asleep fairly quickly.

Suddenly, I was startled awake by the telephone that rang. I wasn't sure if Bernard and Isabelle were home yet, or if they were calling to check in on the kids.

Instinctively, I picked up the phone.

"Bonsoir," I answered.

"Hello, Isabelle, may I please speak with Cheryl?"

Wait. This is my mom, I thought.

I rubbed the sleep out of my eyes.

"Mom, it's me."

By that time, I realized Isabelle was home and she'd picked up the phone in her bedroom.

"Isabelle, it's okay, it's my mom."

I was startled to see it was 1:30 in the morning.

Surely, she's forgotten that there's a 7-hour time difference between us.

"Mom, do you know it's 1:30 in the morning here?"

"Yes, Cheryl, there's been an emergency and we need you to come home right away."

"What is it Mom? Uncle Walter?" I was ready to explain why I couldn't make it home for my uncle's funeral.

"No, Honey, it's your daddy."

"Daddy? What happened to Daddy?"

"Cheryl, your daddy went into cardiac arrest today."

"Is he okay? Where's he at?"

"Cheryl, your daddy is gone," she said softly as she pushed back the tears in her throat.

I didn't understand and continued to fire questions.

"Gone? You mean they've moved him from Elkneck Hospital to Hartford Hospital? Which hospital is he in? Mom, what are you saying?"

"Cheryl, your daddy died today."

"What? Daddy died? When? How?"

I was in shock.

"Cheryl, I found your daddy near the pond in our back yard. It appears he may have had a heart attack and hit his head on the stone around the pond. We need you to come home right away."

"Mom, I hear what you're saying, is someone with you?"

"Yes, Amy's here."

"Can I talk to her?" The next voice I heard was my sister-in-law.

"Amy, is it true? Did my daddy die today?"

"Yes, he did." She gently responded.

I *hurled* the phone receiver across the dining room, and *screamed* and *cried* at the top of my lungs.

"*No, no, not my daddy! Not my daddy, no, noooooo.*"

Isabelle came running down the stairs and grabbed me.

"Chérie, what's wrong?"

"My daddy's dead—my daddy's dead." I cried, I *screamed*.

Isabelle grabbed me by the shoulders and shook me.

"No, Chérie. It's not your daddy; it's your uncle Walter. Your *uncle* died," she tried to assure me.

"No, it's *not* my uncle Walter. *It's my daddy; He's dead. My daddy's dead!*" I fell to my knees, and *screamed*, and *pounded* the floor with my fists.

The phone rang again. I knew it was my mom. Isabelle answered. She wanted to confirm that I'd misunderstood and that it was my uncle Walter who'd died.

"Hello?"

I heard my mom's voice. She was very concerned about me. I heard her tell Isabelle, "Cheryl's daddy died and we need help to get her home right away." Isabelle assured my mom they would help me get on the next flight. She hung up, ran over to me, grabbed my shoulders, looked sternly into my eyes, and said, "Chérie your mom is worried sick about you. She needs you to be strong right now. Call her back and assure her that you're okay. She thinks she needs to send someone to Paris to meet you. Chérie assure her that you'll catch the next flight out and be home right away."

I pulled myself together enough to make the call.

"Mom, I'm so, so sorry, so sorry. I'll catch the next flight out. I'll go straight to the airport and will be home soon. I'm so sorry Mom." I cried softly.

Mom sobbed so hard we ended the call.

Isabelle had a glass of water in hand and gave me a sleeping pill. She forced me to take it. "It'll help you to stay calm until you get home. There's nothing you can do before the airport opens."

Isabelle suggested I pack my bags and try to rest. Bernard would drive me to the airport in the morning. Isabelle went to bed.

I staggered to the bathroom.

I was physically sick.

I was in shock.

I realized that everything in my world had turned upside down in a split second.

I sobbed and sobbed.

I remembered the last time I saw my daddy, six months ago, at my sister's wedding.

I remembered the last time I spoke with my daddy on Christmas Day.

It was March 14, the day my daddy died.

My daddy's dead. I sobbed.

"Why did I give up the last Christmas to be with my daddy?"

I beat myself up.

I was selfish to be away from my family on Christmas. My family needs me and I'm in Paris, thousands of miles away on the worst day of our lives. They're all there grieving, in shock, and I'm so far away. I'm alone.

The "if only" began to haunt me.

I packed my clothes.

I had no intentions of returning to my au pair job and probably not to Paris. My daddy died and I needed to be with my family.

Mel was in Canada for ten days. So, I was completely alone.

This amazing day just became the worst day of my life.

I stayed in my room and grieved my unimaginable loss. I had several hours before I'd leave for the airport. I lay on my bed, thought about this season, how glorious it was and how I'd got my heart back. I'd just told God to send me to the most remote parts of the earth for Him. I'd be His messenger. My heart was in shock—complete and utter shock.

Inside, I was glad that I'd no longer have to wash, dry, and iron fourteen loads of wash, or clean and cook. It was a lot. I wouldn't miss that at all. But, what would happen to my life in God that I'd gained in this season? How would my daddy's death affect that?

Going home was bittersweet.

What will I have to face when I arrive home? What will I do when the funeral is over? Where will I go? Where will I stay?

It's March—I'd have to wait to begin my senior year at the university in the fall.

What will I do for six months?

I knew what I'd gained in this honeymoon season with God could never be taken away from me.

But, how would all of these changes affect me?

These questions pummeled my heart and mind.

I picked up my disc-man and played Kent Henry's *Jeremiah 29:11* CD. I'd gone to sleep listening to this every night during my time in Paris. It comforted me.

I heard Bernard come down the steps.

"Chérie I'm so sorry to hear about your father. We must call the airport straight away. They'd be open now."

He spoke with airline agents, who told him it would be best if we came directly to the airport; then, we'd have a better chance of getting on the next flight out to New York.

We arrived at Charles de Gaulle International Airport. I was one step closer to home even though I was still 3,700 miles away.

Bernard went directly to the powers that be and spoke on my behalf. I felt safe and assured that I'd be on my way home soon.

Within thirty minutes, I was placed on an airplane that was moments away from departure. I had no time to check-in my gigantic, oversized, purple duffle bag. I had to drag it with me on the plane. I was the last one to board.

The male flight attendant, not knowing my situation, was quite annoyed with me for carrying my massive, oversized duffle bag on the plane.

It wouldn't fit in the overhead compartment, under my feet or seat. Frustrated, he finally snatched my heavy burden and disappeared.

I was upset by his insensitivity.

Didn't he know why I was on this flight? It was an emergency, and not just any emergency, my daddy died, Sir. That's why I didn't have time to check in the stupid, duffle bag. At least I'm on the plane and I'm finally going home.

Chapter 7

Finally Home

"God's heart was the first of all our hearts to break."
—William Sloane Coffin

My best friend, Theresa, and her husband drove me home from the airport. It had taken me thirty-six hours, but I was almost there. Five minutes from home, I'd developed a huge knot in my throat. I could barely swallow. My breath was labored, stomach nauseous.

We made a right turn down *Rocky Road*, turned left onto *Brick Road*, and I saw my parents' home—corner lot, lovely yellow ranch house directly in front of me.

I pushed back tears when I saw my daddy's tuxedo black Ford F150, with steel gray and red trim, sitting in the driveway. My heart raced. We pulled into the driveway; I jumped from the car and walked to the carport entrance.

My older brother, Rob, met me at the door. I reached out to embrace him.

"I'm so sorry Rob, I'm so sorry."

I stepped through the door; the air inside was constricted.

I could hardly breathe.

I hugged my younger sister, Laura.

"I'm so sorry Sis, so sorry." I held her tightly.

I tried to push back my tears.

When I saw my mom I couldn't hold them back any longer. I hugged her.

"I'm so sorry Mom, I'm so sorry."

I hugged Grammy and my younger brother, Brian.

"I'm so sorry Brian."

Mom greeted Theresa and her husband. They agreed to stay around for a while.

Five minutes later, Mom called a family meeting.

"I need to talk to my children," which included her daughter and son-in-law, privately in her bedroom.

Theresa, her husband, and Grammy stayed in the living room.

I felt like I was being suffocated. I struggled to breathe.

Someone was missing at this family meeting. It's my daddy, my daddy's not here.

I ached.

Mom closed the bedroom door. Some of us were sitting on the bed and others stood.

"I don't wanna tell you this, but I need to because others know and I don't want you to hear this from anyone else," she began. "A week ago, your daddy and I went to visit uncle Walter in the hospital. As you know, doctors say that uncle Walter has two months to live. When your daddy and I walked out of the hospital last Saturday, he was crying, he looked at me and said, 'I don't want to watch another brother die.'

Monday your dad's truck engine blew up. He was fretting because we didn't have the money to replace it. He wanted to borrow the money to fix his truck. I encouraged him to trust the Lord. I reminded him he had permission to drive his company's truck as long as he needed to.

He was upset and frantic. He got the company truck, but he didn't want to keep it long, and still wanted to borrow money.

The next couple of days were quiet. He was worried. When I realized he was still frantic, I encouraged him to borrow the money if that's what he wanted.

He ran to the telephone and arranged to borrow several thousand dollars the next day.

Your daddy seemed relieved.

On Friday, he came home from work exhausted. I tried to get him to talk. He said he'd been out in the freezing cold weather pouring concrete all day.

Sitting on the toilet he said, 'This is the first time I've been able to go to the bathroom all day.'

I had to go do Mom's hair, but I invited him to come with me so that we could be together.

He said, "no".

I went by myself.

Later that night when I came home he was already in bed.

I crawled in beside him, and tried to be close.

He wouldn't respond, so I just held him.

We went to sleep.

The next morning, your father jumped out of bed.

"Honey, where are you going?"

He told me it was snowing, and that he had to get his truck back to his job.

"Why are you taking your company truck back? You need it for work Monday."

His behavior didn't make any sense.

It was snowing outside, and he's driving forty-five minutes to return his truck to his job.

I tried to get him to talk to me, but he was frantic.

I just let him go and do what he wanted.

He returned home early afternoon.

I didn't like the way he looked in his face, and his behavior was very strange.

"Honey, you're scaring me.

You look like someone who wants to do something to themself.

Talk to me.

What's going on inside?"

It was like pulling teeth to get him to say anything.

Reluctantly, he said he felt like a failure as a husband, a father and provider.

I told him that wasn't true.

I told him that he was a good man, a gentle and kind man and that's why I married him.

I told him that he'd been a good father and provider.

I was so worried.

I asked him questions and he wouldn't respond.

The look on his face scared me. So, I prayed for him right there. I asked God to assure your daddy that everything was going to be all right.

I told him I was going to make lunch.

I pulled a frozen pizza out of the freezer and put it in the oven.

Your daddy went to the basement.

After a few minutes, I went to tell him the pizza would be ready soon.

As I came down the stairs, I saw your daddy kneeling down in front of the sliding glass doors.

His back was to me.

When he heard my steps he turned and glanced over his right shoulder.

Thank God, he's praying; he's crying out to the Lord, I thought.

I didn't want to interrupt that moment so I went upstairs.

Fifteen minutes later the pizza was finished; I sat down at the kitchen table to eat. I figured your daddy would come up when he was ready.

As I was sitting at the kitchen table, I looked out our bay window at the pond.

Wait a minute.

I looked again, this time straining my eyes to see what in the world was in our pond.

It looked like the shirt your daddy was wearing.

I ran out the back door, and peered over the embankment.

Sure enough, it was your dad's shirt.

I ran down the embankment, up to the pond, and saw your daddy face down in the pond.

I didn't know what'd happened.

I tried to pull him out.

He was heavy, wet, and I struggled.

I yelled for help and ran back into the house to call 911.

They told me how to get the water out of him and how to get him to start breathing again.

I tried and tried," crying, she continued.

"It took them *soooo* long to get here.

The paramedics took too long.

I did everything I could.

Finally, the ambulance arrived.

They cut the shirt off your daddy, and tried to resuscitate him. But, they couldn't.

They put him in the ambulance and took him to the hospital. He was pronounced dead on arrival.

Once we got inside the hospital and they had your daddy's clothes off of him, we noticed a bruise on his head. We noticed cuts in his wrists and wounds in his chest that indicated that your daddy might have done this to himself.

I had to go to the police station to be questioned.

It felt like an interrogation.

They kept me for three hours until they had enough evidence that confirmed that your daddy intended to commit suicide."

I was shocked. *Did my mom just say that my daddy committed suicide? Suicide?*

Mom continued.

"The police had your daddy's wallet.

They found the check that was given him to fix his truck inside. They also found a receipt that showed he transferred the money from his individual account into our joint account. This proved to the police that your daddy premeditated his steps.

I'm sorry.

I didn't want to tell you this, but I knew someone would.

Your daddy drowned. He committed suicide."

I don't remember anything my mom said after those words.

I was shocked.

I hugged my siblings, and said the only thing you can say, "I'm so sorry."

I left my parents' bedroom, pulled my friends outside, and told them, "My daddy died by suicide. He drowned himself."

They said they were sorry, profusely, and said they had to leave.

I went inside the house; it was suffocating.

I couldn't breathe.

My heart pounded and threatened to explode into a million pieces.

Suddenly, I felt robbed.

I felt like Death walked right into our home and stole my daddy.

He was gone.

He wasn't ever coming back.

I didn't know what to think.

I didn't know what to say.

I didn't know how to respond.

I just shook my head, and caught the tears before they trickled down my already tear-stained cheeks.

My siblings and I looked at each other and simply shook our heads in shock and disbelief.

How does a faithful Christian man of more than 30 years die by suicide? He was just in church on Thursday evening, and Saturday he's dead—by his own hand. This doesn't make sense.

I began to search for answers to the mysterious question— WHY? I had to admit as a Christian for 25 years, I'd struggled with major depression and suicide only two years earlier. I understood that it's quite possible for a Believer to become so discouraged and depressed, that suicide could seem tempting. I'd been there. I knew it was possible.

In an effort to offer comfort to my distraught siblings, I told them that I'd struggled with major depression and suicide two years earlier. I told them I understood how Daddy could simply just be overwhelmed by the struggle, and no longer had the energy to fight—not even for one more day.

My younger brother told us that he too, at one point in his life had struggled with thoughts of suicide. Then, my older brother acknowledged that he too has had to ignore suicidal thoughts in the past. My sister admitted that she too had thoughts of despair and hopelessness at one point in her life.

I was shocked.

We were shocked.

We'd never shared this with each other, *ever*.

We never talked about this *S*-word.

My family never knew that I'd suffered with major depression, and was hospitalized for a suicide attempt only two years earlier.

At the time I was 25 and I threatened to sue anyone who told my parents I was in the hospital for a suicide attempt.

I hadn't told any of them.

I began to wonder how many people really struggle with suicidal ideas—relentless, tormenting thoughts of ending their life. *Is this common, or is death hovering over my family and tempting us with suicide?*

Chapter 8

The Funeral

"When we honestly ask ourselves which person in our lives means the most to us, we often find that it is those who, instead of giving advice, solutions, or cures, have chosen rather to share our pain and touch our wounds with a warm and tender hand."
—Henry Nouwen

The funeral service was just two days after I'd arrived home. This whole experience was a whirlwind. I hardly knew what to think. I absolutely dreaded this night. I did not want to see my daddy dead. I didn't want to see him lying in a casket at the altar of the church.

This was his church for nearly three decades. He helped build and maintain it. He raised his family on the front row of this church.

I didn't know how I was going to make it through the service. I couldn't anticipate what my response would or should be.

The church strongly believed that to die by suicide was a sin. And this sin was called murder. And the penalty for this self-murderous act was Hell.

I was troubled by my daddy's thought process. I didn't believe he'd gone to Hell. But, he would've believed that he was going there based on the church's belief on suicide. *Why would he choose Hell?*

This was a disturbing thought.

Nearly 1,000 friends, family, co-workers, and community members came to pay their respects, and to honor my daddy and his family for the impact he'd made in each of their lives.

It was surreal to sit and look at him. I couldn't believe this moment was happening. Most of the evening was a blur. Everyone stared at the family, and watched our responses during the service.

What I enjoyed the most about my daddy's funeral service were the songs.

My daddy loved lighthouses. And he loved songs about them. One of his favorite songs was *The Lighthouse*. My junior-high Sunday school teacher sung the song in memory of him.

The sanctuary choir sang one of my favorite songs, Vicki Yohe's song, *Mercy Seat*. And that's just what I was doing. I was runnin' to the Mercy Seat with all of my heart, soul, mind and strength, and asking God to let my daddy find His mercy and grace. I prayed that He'd look beyond my daddy's final act, and that He'd take into account the way my daddy faithfully lived and served Him all his days.

Another favorite song sung that night was a personal request of mine. I requested that my best friend, Theresa, sing, *His Strength Is Perfect* by CeCe Winan's.

And by God's amazing grace, we made it through my daddy's funeral service.

I said goodbye to my daddy's body.

I kissed his bruised head.

I touched his hand. But he wasn't there. It was just a very cold almost plastic-like shell of him.

A couple of my family members cried uncontrollably.

We closed the lid on my daddy's stainless steel casket, watched as the pallbearers carried my daddy's body in a box, and placed it inside the undertaker's car—a silver hearse.

We would meet the next morning at the gravesite to bury my daddy.

Burial Day

Ashes to ashes—dust to dust, I placed a red rose on my daddy's coffin. I watched as it was lowered into the ground.

The weather best described the ache of that moment for me. It was a very dreary, gray, dark, cold and wet day. It'd been raining.

I felt robbed in so many ways. I had so many questions and very few answers, if any.

The burial was short, but not so sweet.

We returned to my parents' home where friends served our family into mid-afternoon.

I hated that day.

I hated everything about that day.

I hated every conversation about that day.

I was angry when I heard people laughing in our home that afternoon.

How could they laugh? My daddy was dead.

He died by suicide.

Our family is in crisis, people!

This is not funny.

But, I reminded myself that most people thought my daddy had a heart attack and died. This was done to protect the honor and dignity of my dad, and to protect our family from the stigma associated with suicide. And, to be absent from the body, was to be present with Christ, and what a glorious and blessed hope.

Except, the way my daddy died was anything but glorious or blessed.

It was sudden.

It was tragic.

It was traumatic.

It was violent.

It was simply awful.

I felt that the whole world should stop, have at least one day of silence, fast, and mourn my daddy's tragic death.

At last, one of the worst days of my life had come to an end. Everyone had gone.

They left us with many cards, warm sympathies, beautiful flowers, green plants and tons of food.

But what about the deep hole in the heart of the now widowed wife, four children, siblings, in-laws and granddaughter?

You can fill a burial hole in a matter of a few minutes, but how will we address the gigantic gaping hole in our hearts?

Chapter 9

Broken Heart

"Mental pain is less dramatic than physical pain, but it is more common and also more hard to bear. The frequent attempt to conceal mental pain increases the burden: it is easier to say, "My tooth is aching" than to say "My heart is broken."
—C.S. Lewis

The days that followed were very hard.
I didn't want to eat.
I'd go into my daddy's closets and smell him.
I sniffed his clothes; both dress clothes and work clothes.
There were two distinctive scents.
I stared at my daddy's tall stainless steel thermos, his red lunch box, and his yellow work hat.
I stared at his black truck.
Inside my heart was hemorrhaging.
How would we survive this traumatic blow to our hearts?
We had no grid for this kind of pain.
We had no preparation for this sort of tragedy and trauma.
There seemed to be no one who could really help us.
We were given no coping resources.
We were left alone to pick up the pieces of our broken hearts.

It was like trying to pick up the pieces from a shattered family picture. There were a thousand pieces of tiny glass shards.

Nothing would ever be the same.

No family picture would ever look quite right.

No holiday would ever feel normal—*normal* was gone forever, and *strange* was here to stay.

A week after my daddy was buried, my mom ventured out for a lunch date with two very dear friends of hers and Dad. When she returned, I saw a look in her eyes that terrified me.

I was petrified.

Her eyes were dark, and swollen from the trauma of the last week. She was in so much pain.

I was the grieving daughter who'd lost her daddy suddenly and tragically. I was hurting. I could only help my mom so much. I couldn't imagine the shock, and horror she was reliving day after day.

But, the look I saw in her eyes caused me to shutter with fear. In that moment, I felt that I'd actually lost both of my parents'. *Mom would never be the same without Daddy.*

When I looked at my mother's eyes, I was nearly convinced that she was being tempted to drive her car over a cliff, or off a bridge somewhere, to end the emotional pain she was in.

But, I wouldn't ask the question.

The belief was that if you talked about suicide, and the person wasn't thinking about it, then you might have planted suicidal ideas into their mind. Maybe they would now consider it, or worse, act on it. I was scared to death my mom wanted to die, too.

I understand now, that belief is only a myth, and research has proven differently.

In those early days, I felt like I'd lost both of my parents'. I felt they'd both died, one physically, the other emotionally. I was terrified that at her core Mom would never be the same. *How could she ever be the same person? How could she overcome?*

I had no intentions of going back to Paris. I couldn't.

My heart was in so much pain.

I was living at home with my mom, and planned to go back to the university in the fall.

What would I do with my days?

I hadn't lived at home for at least seven years.

I went to church with my mom, to be with her, to protect her and so she wouldn't feel so alone.

I couldn't help but remember my daddy lying in a coffin at the altar directly in front of me.

I relived it every time.

I'd stare at the beautiful blue baptismal wall my daddy created.

I didn't like being there.

I no longer shared the beliefs of the church.

I was there for one reason—my mom.

It was so awkward.

This was my parents' family.

This is where they'd poured their blood, sweat and tears.

They'd faithfully given their love, time, service, and hearts.

Now it seemed that my mother had a contagious disease—there was so much *dis-EASE* around her.

By this point, a lot of people heard through the rumor mill that my daddy died by suicide.

People didn't know how to act around her.

They didn't know what to say to her.

It was awkward.

Chapter 10
Complicated Grief

"Distance never separates two hearts that really care, for our memories span the miles and in seconds we are there. But whenever I start feeling sad because I miss you I remind myself how lucky I am to have someone so special to miss."
—Henry Nouwen

In September, I moved back to residence life at the university. I transferred twelve language and culture credits for my rendezvous in Paris.

It was my senior year.

I was somewhat excited.

Because of my age, I was classified a non-traditional student.

I struggled emotionally with the loss of my daddy, and found it difficult to stay focused on almost anything—least of all, school.

I really needed someone to talk to. My best friend, Theresa, recommended that I talk to her counselor, Kathy about my daddy's death. I did.

In September, I began grief counseling with Kathy, a beautiful Canadian woman in her 50's. It had been six months since my daddy died.

She was sincere, empathetic and deeply compassionate.
The first couple of visits were hard because I had to tell the story of my daddy's death.

It was necessary if I was going to receive help.

Initially, I left counseling sessions more sad than I was when I'd arrived. There was so much to explore, so many depths and layers around my father's death by suicide, and the effects it was having on me.

The American Psychiatric Association compared the trauma of losing a loved one to suicide with a catastrophic event such as suffering in a concentration camp.

Intense!

It was complicated all right.

I didn't have many friends at the university. However, my best friend, Theresa was a Residence Director on campus. I did have the good fortune to visit her home as often as I needed. She was always a source of comfort.

I decided to go back to my church in Philadelphia. I went most Sundays. But, it wasn't the same. I wasn't the same, I'd moved forward. I'd been away for a year and this wasn't a typical year.

I had grown in my faith tremendously.

In the wisdom of God, maybe He drew me close to Him to prepare my heart for the upcoming trauma I would encounter. My relationship with Him was different.

I could no longer endure what I felt was a theatrical performance Sunday after Sunday. I needed more—so much more.

I was part of the church's ministerial; therefore, I had to sit on the platform each Sunday.

I saw people differently.

I saw pain on their faces.

I saw the struggles they went through.

It pained me when I remembered my daddy was in his church on a Thursday night, and dead the next Saturday afternoon. A cry began to arise out of the core of my being—there *must be* more than this, oh God!

I could no longer settle for church as usual.

I could no longer listen to recycled sermons.

I needed something more.

I believed the people needed something more, too, if they were to have the coping resources to overcome life's challenges and crises.

I talked to my counselor about this heart pain, and the challenge I'd been having. Kathy would never tell me what to do. Instead, she listened, and asked questions.

One Sunday, I was sitting on the platform alongside the other Ministers as Pastor gave his sermon.

The congregation was rather non-responsive that morning.

In this black church, the preacher needed somebody to talk back to him. So, he spun around, and looked to his Ministers.

"I know my ministers better say 'Amen.'"

He commanded us to stand to our feet and to talk back to him.

For instance: "Amen, Bishop, PREACH! You betta preach Bishop. C'mon now, tell it like it is! Well! Alright, you're talking now, Pastor."

As is the cultural expression in some black churches, the Hammond B-3 organ had to talk back, too.

I took my seat, turned to my friend and said, "This is my last Sunday in this church and I will not be back."

I couldn't watch peoples emotions get all stirred up, and leave the service saying, "My didn't we have a shoutin' good time today?" And on Monday morning, have no ability to cope with the circumstances life served them.

I was tired of church. I loved God with all of my heart, but once again, I was tired of *doing church*. I had no intentions of finding another one anytime soon, *if ever*.

I loved my relationship with God. I just needed to be in a place where my heart could heal fully—where the whole man would be addressed, not spiritual needs alone, but body, soul and spirit.

First Holidays

I dreaded the holidays. I wished we could've just passed over them—you know, skipped all of them!

The first year of the *new normal*, holidays were so very painful. We carried on as best we could. Perhaps, people who didn't know us wouldn't discern the hidden pain behind the smile, and in the eyes of most of our holiday photos.

We all dreaded the first Christmas after daddy died.

We didn't know quite how or what to *celebrate*.

We didn't feel like celebrating at all.

There seemed to be a knife in my chest Christmas day.

The day couldn't end fast enough.

Just when I thought grief couldn't possibly get more complicated than the loss of a parent to suicide, *it did*.

First Anniversary

My daddy died in the winter, in March. When February came, I spent the whole month dreading March, specifically the week of March 14.

When that dreaded morning arrived, I relived all the events.

I saw my daddy struggling with his decision.

I saw him drive to his job on that snowy Saturday morning.

I envisioned him transferring his savings into my parents' joint checking account, and closing his individual one.

I relived the conversations that Mom had with Dad.

I relived his responses.

I relived every single detail of that tragic day.

I relived the entire week.

And to make it even more difficult, I had a videotape of his funeral. I'd watch it over and over. I still don't know if it was helpful or not, but, it's what I needed to do in that moment.

My counselor, Kathy, did the kindest thing for me on that snowy anniversary day. She picked me up in her adorable, green Jeep Wrangler, and drove me to a warm, comfy cozy café, just to be with me. She gave me a card expressing sincere sympathy and encouragement. It meant the world to me and helped me through that terrible day—the first year anniversary.

Graduation

I earned a B.A. in Elementary Education with a minor in Social Work.

How I ever made it through the semester and down the aisle wearing my gown, hat and tassel, I'll never know. I strongly suspect it was *only* the grace of God.

It was a great achievement, but it was an awkward day. Neither Mom nor Dad could celebrate with me—he was gone. Mom had just sold their home and moved to North Carolina. I understood why she needed to leave. She had to heal, and the best way for her, she felt, was to move out-of-state.

Second Anniversary

After graduation, I began to feel more despondent about my life. Who was I? Where was I going? And how was I going to get there?

When you graduate you continue your education, or you get a job, preferably in the field you've studied. But, I never wanted to teach math, English, science or social studies in an elementary school. I wanted to help troubled youth. I thought I'd do guidance counseling in the schools, and earn a counseling degree. But, my heart was still in too much pain. It took every ounce of energy just to get up every day.

I was approaching the second anniversary of my daddy's death. You'd think it would've been easier than the first, but it wasn't. It was just as difficult.

January came, and I felt sick knowing the second anniversary of my daddy's death would soon be here. I was becoming more and more depressed. I began to struggle with thoughts of suicide again—the emotional pain was far greater than I could manage.

One week, the thoughts of suicide became so powerful that I had to see or talk to my counselor every single day.

She insisted that I sign a *Commitment To Safety Form*, which simply said, that I promised not to attempt suicide and would call for help first.

My best friend, Theresa, asked me to come stay with her until the suicidal feelings abated. So, I did.

Where do you think the first place she wanted to take me was?

To her new church—you gotta know, that's the last place I wanted to be.

Theresa was so excited about her church, pastors and new family. She said her pastors were professional counselors and they offered a holistic approach to ministry.

I was happy she was happy, but I didn't want to be involved. I begged and pleaded to stay home or to wait in the car, to no avail, I was on *suicide watch*. I had no choice.

When we arrived at the church, she walked right up to the front row. Inside I screamed, *"I hate this. I don't wanna be here!"*

The pastor did not speak that night. Instead, a female minister spoke. When she got up to speak, in my heart I said, *that woman has nothing to say to me.* I tried not to pay attention, though I admired her skillful delivery. In her closing remarks, she introduced a mime dance. When I heard the music, I thought, *Wait a minute. I know that song. I use to sing it on ministry trips during my Bible college days. God, that's our song. Why are you letting me hear this song? Why now?*

Suddenly, uncontrollable tears cascaded down my cheeks. I doubled over and sobbed. The song was *Stubborn Love* by Kathy Troccoli.

It's Your stubborn love. It never let's go of me. I don't understand, how You could stay. Perfect love, embracing the worst in me. I can't live without Your stubborn love.

In that moment, I didn't know how, but I knew that I desperately needed to lean into the embrace of God's *stubborn love*. He had proved that, "If I ascend to heaven, You are there; If I make my bed in Sheol, You are there." (Psalm 139:8)

The next thing I knew, the pastors and the entire church gathered around me. They prayed and prophesied into my life. I made a recommitment, in that moment, to lean into Love's embrace and *chose* to live.

I wish I could tell you the next day I didn't have suicidal thoughts. But, I did. In fact, they increased and intensified for two more weeks.

Every minute, of every day, I fought to stay alive. I wanted the unrelenting, tormenting emotional pain to stop assaulting my heart and mind.

What was I going to do? I decided to take the pain of my heart and to lean into His *Stubborn Love.*

Chapter 11

The Bonfire

"The past does not have to be your prison. You have a
voice in your destiny. You have a say in your life. You
have a choice in the path you take."
—Max Lucado

Thank God, March was over!

Two months had passed since Love had invited me out of my
closet of pain, and drew me into His strong embrace.

I'd begun to sense the Lord asking me to get rid of all the *stuff*
I'd accumulated over the last several years—depressing journals,
books, funeral pictures and video; things that I would frequently
look at, and read, that led me to despair of life.

I'd thought I would eventually publish much of what I'd written
in those journals, so I asked the Lord. *Are these thoughts the Devil's,
Yours, Lord or mine*? I had to know.

I dropped to my knees, picked up my Bible, and asked Jesus to
confirm if this was He leading me. I let my Bible open to whatever
page it desired, Isaiah 30. My eyes landed on verse 18, and I began
to read.

Therefore the LORD longs to be gracious to you, And therefore
He waits on high to have compassion on you. For the LORD is
a God of justice; How blessed are all those who long for Him. O

people in Zion…you will weep no longer. He will surely be gracious to you at the sound of your cry; when He hears it, He will answer you. Although, the Lord has given you bread of privation (hardship, adversity) and the water of oppression, He, your Teacher, will no longer hide Himself, but your eyes will behold your Teacher. And your ears will hear a word behind you saying…this is the way, walk in it…and you will defile your graven images overlaid with silver, and your molten images plated with gold. You will scatter them as an impure thing; and say to them, BE GONE!

(Is. 30:18-22, parenthetical added)

I knew God was telling me that those funeral pictures, depressing writings, and video had become graven images. I spent hours and hours, days, and months ruminating and reminiscing the darkest season of my life. This always led me into another depressive episode.

God was asking me to destroy these graven images. This revelation pierced my heart and I sobbed, not because it was great revelation, but because I was already mourning the loss of those things.

In obedience I took it all to a friend's house. We carried books, photo albums, composition notebooks, journals, the video of my daddy's funeral, and placed it, piece by piece, into her fire pit! It took nearly two hours for the fire to consume years of darkness and pain. In fact, the Lord spoke to me during the bonfire.

"You see these things burning up naturally? I'm also burning the effects of these graven images from your soul and spirit. No longer will the pain, and the stigma haunt you. I'm burning it up!"

The bonfire was an act of obedience on my part, driven by my love for Him. I expected nothing in return. I simply wanted to love Him that way.

To my great surprise, I experienced staggering peace, unspeakable joy, and sheer delight. There was a song in my heart, praise on my lips, and a skip in my step. I was so happy.

It had been *years* since I'd experienced such happy emotions.

Right away, I felt God's smile from Heaven as He looked at me. I felt His acceptance of my burnt offering, if you will. He honored His word, and my gift of love.

When the bonfire ceased to burn, only ashes remained. Another fire was burning—the fire of His desire for me. His love filled me. I knew He was pleased with my obedience. I gave Him what was most precious, and most valuable to me—the pain of my heart.

I would have been forever grateful to Him, if only the torment of those memories no longer haunted me. That would have been *more* than enough.

But, He did so much more than He had promised. Not only did He remove the insidious effects of darkness from a heart consumed with sorrow, grief and pain. He gave me the Isaiah 61 experience—A Divine Exchange.

He gave me authentic joy—the oil of gladness instead of mourning. He gave me a mantle of praise instead of the spirit of despair. He gave me a crown of beauty instead of ashes. (Is. 61:3, NIV) He gave me a double portion blessing. What an astonishing exchange!

My journey toward healing had begun!

My Goodbye Song:

Daddy, I Forgive You
When I heard the news that you left me
I could barely see
Tears blinded me
I screamed
And I cried
For what seemed like hours
Saying, "No, no, not my daddy
Come back, Daddy
Wake up, Daddy
Don't leave me
I need you Daddy
We'll get through this
We always have

We always will
This season won't last forever
Please Daddy
Don't go."

But, Momma said,
"I'm sorry. Your daddy's gone."

I couldn't believe my ears
I couldn't believe you were gone
You didn't say goodbye
You didn't tell me something was desperately wrong
Daddy, I forgive you.

When you went away
And you chose not to stay
Cause you thought this was the only way out of your pain
Daddy, I forgive you.

For when you said
"I quit
I can't take this anymore
There's no use of trying
I'm outta here
I'm gone"
Daddy, I forgive you.

For my last memory
The haunting images you left me
For leaving me this painful legacy
Daddy, I forgive you.

For special moments you've missed
For every picture you're not in
Reminds me of why I have this deep ache inside
Daddy, I forgive you.

I miss your great big smile
I miss your warm embrace
I miss your tender kiss on my forehead, on my face
Daddy, I forgive you.

I miss your sky blue eyes
Those special tears that you cried
I wish you were here
But I've resolved that you're gone
Daddy, I forgive you.

Ebb and flow of the journey.

Oh the kindness of God! I love the way He leads and shepherds our hearts in love. He showed me a way out of the continual tailspin of despair and hopelessness. He gave me a huge leap forward on my journey of healing.

And, it is a journey, with five steps forward, and two steps back, at times. Healing is a process and takes time. During this process, we learn how to navigate the ebbs and flows of the healing journey.

Inevitably, though, an unexpected situation or circumstance would trigger me on this journey. A barrage of negative thoughts and feelings would again assault my mind. Bitterness and anger knocked at my heart's door, and tempted me to let them come back and visit for a day or two.

Sometimes I gave in. But, with them came pain, sorrow and despair. Joy and peace were nowhere to be found. In just a few hours, I'd feel depressed and wanted only to crawl up in my bed, curl up like a baby, pull the blanket of despair up over my eyes and sleep.

But I didn't like the way I felt, lethargic and unhappy. So, I'd put a time limit on it—something a wise counselor encouraged me to do. I allowed myself to feel whatever it was that I felt, for a day or two, max.

Eventually I'd examine why I felt angry or sad. I wrote down all the reasons. Sometimes, I needed to let go of a real or perceived injustice, and simply forgive someone—my dad, the church, a pastor, a family member, or a friend.

I've learned that forgiveness, too, was a process. I made a choice to forgive or not to forgive. Sometimes, in my humanity, I forgave but needed to forgive that person again, when triggered.

When I became aware that I needed to forgive someone, but didn't have the power, strength or desire to do so, I practiced the art of remembrance. I began to think about the very first words Jesus uttered on the cross—"Father, forgive them; for they know not what they are doing." (Luke 23:34)

I believe Jesus asked His Father to forgive every person who cried, "Crucify Him!" To forgive every soldier who had physically helped nail His hands and feet to the cross, and to forgive every transgressor that would ever live. "Father, forgive them; for they know not what they are doing."

In Matthew 6:14, Jesus said, "For if you forgive others for their transgressions, your heavenly Father will also forgive you."

There's a prerequisite. In order for me to ask God to forgive my transgressions, I must forgive others' transgressions against me.

Well, already in my life, I had a long list of personal transgressions against God and man that I had to deal with.

Many times I'd asked others to forgive me, as well as God. And they forgave me.

So, I learned one way out of the tailspin, one way to free my toxic heart was to choose to say,

"God, forgive them, for they know not what they're doing."*

*Grit teeth and repeat as necessary!

Chapter 12

My Father

"An infinite God can give all of Himself to each of His
children. He does not distribute Himself that each may
have a part, but to each one He gives all of Himself as
fully as if there were no others."
—A.W. Tozer

I was having some quality time with God one afternoon. I sensed
that He wanted me to call Him "Father."

*You have more than 300 names, God. Is it really that big a deal if
I choose NOT to call You "Father?" I'm just trying to have some quality
time here. Why are we getting stuck on this? I'm ready to move on to
other things. You know, the things I want to talk about.*

The invitation came again.

I was quite annoyed by His gentle persistence on this issue.

"I want you to call Me Father."

"Why?" I screamed.

"What's the big deal? Father holds many painful feelings, and
images for me. I can't say it, and not think about, or see my earthly
father's face. And, that image brings back painful memories."

When my daddy was alive I'd always called him "dad" or
"daddy," never "father!" I knew he was my father, but his name was
Daddy.

The day he died I called my best friend, Theresa. In her thick Brooklyn accent she responded, "Your Faaaather?"

"Yes, my Father!"

I've never forgotten the sound and the pain of those words. Initially, it was the pain of loss and separation.

I didn't get to say goodbye.

There'd be no more hugs from my daddy.

I'd never see him smile or laugh again.

He wouldn't walk me down the proverbial aisle.

This was the initial pain associated with my daddy's death. Of course, this is before I knew the whole story—how he really died.

My daddy, a Christian man who served God to the best of his ability for nearly 30 years, died by suicide. He chose to end his life violently—forever altering, crippling, and distorting the image, and the meaning of the title, "Father."

When I heard "Father," I immediately, like many people, felt abandoned, unsafe, unprotected, and unloved.

My father left me.

He never consulted me.

He never warned me.

He chose to leave forever.

He had no ability to fight the demons of self-pity, despair and hopelessness.

He left.

He decided he didn't want to be here anymore.

Did he even think about me before he died?

Was I a thought or consideration?

Did he have any idea how much pain his loss would be for me?

I know his body was tired from decades of hard physical labor.

I know he was fatigued.

I know he'd lost a brother only two years earlier.

I understand he was told that his brother was diagnosed with a terminal disease and was given two months to live.

I know he gave all of his "free" time serving others and his church.

There was always something someone wanted my dad to do.

He was tired.

I know he didn't feel successful as a father.

Maybe, in my daddy's mind, all of his children were backslidden. According to his beliefs, that meant he'd failed as a father.

I know that he was financially strapped, and when his truck engine blew up, he had no financial means to replace it.

But couldn't he have continued fighting for me?

Wasn't the thought of walking me down the aisle enough?

What about protecting my mom?

Wasn't that enough?

What about his granddaughter, and the other grandbabies that would soon follow?

If he lost everything, he still had everything, didn't he?

Did my father have to reject and abandon all of us?

That's why I'd rather call You "LORD," than call You "Father." I'd rather call You "Holy One," than call You "Father." I would rather call You "Faithful," than call You "Father." I'll call You "Sovereign," but don't make me call You "Father!"

And, that was the end of my quality time with God that day.

I sounded quite self-absorbed, but I needed Him to see my perspective. I needed to be understood.

One day God asked me a surprising question. I was surprised because I believed God knew ALL things. I believed He was omniscient. But on this day, I wondered if perhaps God just might be having a *senior moment*.

"Cheryl, where did you come from?"

"Uh, where did I come from God? You really don't know? Well, I came from my dad's loins and from my mother's womb! That's where I came from. I mean surely You must know about the birds and the bees, God! Remember, You created the anatomy with a strategy, right? I mean, husband and wife come together in holy marital union, and with proper use of their respective unique parts, they can make a baby!"

Then, more surprisingly, God asked another question.

"Cheryl, where did man come from?"

I understood He was asking about the first man and woman. In an effort to be sensitive to His *senior moment*, I mean after all, He must be a gazillion years old by now. I responded.

"God? Well, do You remember the first week of creation?

On the first day, You created the heavens and the earth, light and darkness, night and day. Remember?

On the second, day You separated the waters above from the waters below and the expanse above, You called Heaven.

And on the third day, You gathered the waters below together and called them seas. Then, dry ground appeared and You called forth vegetation, plants yielding seed, and trees bearing fruit after their kind. Remember?"

I went on to remind Him of the fourth, fifth and the sixth day creation narrative.

"And to finally answer Your question, on the sixth day, You also created man in Your own image and likeness; male and female, and they, too, were made to reproduce.

You know, the birds and the bee's thing I reminded You of earlier!"

Suddenly, a drip drop of revelation trickled into my tiny little brain slower than saline solution into an IV. Stuttering, I said, "Wait? Man, made in Your likeness and in Your image, came from You!

Man, came from You!

Man, came from You?

Oh, I get it!

You created man!

You made man to reproduce, but You create man!

Yeah, I do seem to remember Psalm 139 saying something about this!" I reached for my Bible and read verses 13-16:

For You formed my inward parts; You wove me in my mother's womb. I will give thanks to You, for I am fearfully and wonderfully made; wonderful are Your works, And my soul knows it very well. My frame was not hidden from You when I was made in secret, and skillfully wrought in the depths of the earth; Your eyes have seen my unformed substance, and in Your book were all written the days that were ordained for me, when as yet there was none.

My jaw dropped and my eyes quadrupled in size.

"Well, they certainly didn't tell me this when I learned about those birds and bees.

You *are* my Father!

You're my Father!

Oh yeah!

The Lord's Prayer says something about that, too, I think!"

I found Matthew, chapter 6, and quickly located the famous prayer Jesus taught his disciples. Oh my goodness, I hadn't found the prayer yet, but look, Jesus said this in verse one.

Beware of practicing your righteousness before men to be noticed by them; otherwise you have no reward with *your Father who is in heaven*. (emphasis added)

Wow, it's right here.

It's not even in black and white.

It's written in red.

I was always taught the red words were the ones you needed to pay attention to.

Well, let me read on and try to find this prayer.

Lo and behold, verse four is written in red, too.

So that your giving will be in secret; and *your Father* who sees what is done in secret will reward you. (emphasis added)

I was fascinated and continued to read.

Jesus was using His red words to talk about the prayer in verse six.

I was always taught that to make the Bible meaningful and personal, that I should personalize the scripture with my name.

Cheryl, when you pray, go into your inner room, close your door and pray to your Father who is in secret, and your Father who sees what is done in secret will reward you, Cheryl. And, when you are praying Cheryl, do not use meaningless repetition as the Gentiles do, for they suppose that they will be heard for their many words. So do not be like them; for your Father knows what you need before you ask Him. Pray, then, in this way: My Father who is in heaven…

I fell to my knees, buried my face in my hands, and cried like a baby.

"I have a Father!

My Father is God!

He lives in Heaven.

I'm His daughter!

I'm *not* a fatherless child anymore, I'm *not* a fatherless child."

I sobbed and sobbed.

I felt my Father, who is in Heaven, reach down and embrace me. Gently, He pulled my head close to His chest and His arms of strength surrounded me.

He kissed my forehead, and then wiped tears away from my eyes. His relentless love gave me stability and security.

I no longer had to be on this emotional rollercoaster with all of its ups, downs, sudden twists and turns.

This exhilarating revelation was an anchor for my floundering fatherless heart. It began to anchor my soul in truth. This truth—the revelation that God is my Father, changed my reality.

It changed everything!

It was a dramatic and unfathomable declaration of my identity, dignity, value and worth. Creator of everything seen and unseen, He's my Father, my daddy, He's not just Creator, He's a lover at His core. He had revealed Himself to me in a way that awakened love inside of me.

Many of you reading this book have had deeply negative experiences with your earthly father. Many of you have not experienced the tender touch of a loving dad.

This void is a great source of pain that compels you to look for love in all the wrong places. You look for love in so many different faces and relationships.

Beware—the devil seeks to use the pain of your unfulfilled longing to confuse you, to deceive you, and to distort your image of a father. His ultimate goal is to keep you from desiring to search for your real father, your heavenly Father. Satan never wants your heart to know or connect with the truth about your Father in Heaven.

You were created to know your Father, and to be in relationship with Him.

Instead, Satan wants you to seek to fulfill your legitimate longing, to know that you are loved and enjoyed by your Father, in wrong ways.

A romantic relationship cannot fill this longing.

Close friendships will never fill this longing.

Financial stability will never fill this longing in your heart.

It never can and never will.

Why?

Because that longing has your Father's name on it and only He can fill it. Every human heart, fatherless or not, was created with this longing.

Sure, I still experience the painful loss of my beloved earthly father. I still feel the absence of my earthly father every Father's Day, holiday and anniversary. I miss him *so* much. My family pictures still prove that someone is gone and someone is missing—it's my earthly father.

But, my heart is anchored to truth, and the reality that my Father in Heaven is not MIA.

He hasn't left me, rejected me or abandoned me.

He's here—present, and actively involved in my life.

He will never leave me, nor forsake me.

His Stubborn Love will never let go of me.

I am His, He owns everything I see and cannot see.

I am His daughter.

Our hearts are unsettled and broken until we know the embrace of our Father who is in Heaven.

Part Two

A Message of Hope

Chapter 13

Finding Meaning in Suffering

"Between stimulus and response there is a space. In that
space is our power to choose our response. In our response
lies our growth and freedom."
— Viktor Frankl

I am often asked these questions, "Why so much pain? Does God
hate me? Did I do something to tick Him off?"

You've gotta know, that I've asked these same questions. Here's
what I've come to learn on the journey toward healing.

One of the greatest temptations we face as humans is the urge
to find immediate relief from our pain. The most common thing we
do in the middle, or after the crisis, is to run from the pain in search
of relief, comfort or pleasure—at any cost.

We all have something or someone we run to when we're in pain
and need to be comforted.

Take a moment to answer the following questions:

What do you use to anesthetize your heart's pain?

Where do you go to find relief for your despairing soul?

Who do you turn to when your heart is hurting to receive
comfort?

What comfort foods do you like to eat when you're sad?

The Big Questions

Pain causes us to ask important questions, and gives us an opportunity to understand the big picture.

What is life about, anyway?
Who am I?
Who loves me?
Who wants me?
Who needs me?
Who really cares about me?
What's the point of life?
Is there more to life than this?

A Principle Of Life

God produces the sun and the rain; and yes, there are seasons where there is sometimes more sunshine and less rain. A prolonged season of sun, without rain, may lead to a drought. A prolonged season of rain, without sunshine, may lead to emotional floods. And in some climates there are seasons of monsoon rains.

And this is the way of life.

Solomon reminds us, that God causes the sun and the rain, to fall on the just and unjust alike.

TO EVERYTHING THERE IS A SEASON, and a time for every matter or purpose under heaven: A time to be born and a time to die, a time to plant and a time to pluck up what is planted, A time to kill and a time to heal, a time to break down and a time to build up, A time to weep and a time to laugh, a time to mourn and a time to dance, A time to cast away stones and a time to gather stones together, a time to embrace and a time to refrain from embracing, A time to get and a time to lose, a time to keep and a time to cast away, A time to rend and a time to sew, a time to keep silence and a time to speak, A time to love and a time to hate, a time for war and a time for peace. (Ecl. 3:1–8, Amplified, emphasis added)

Life has seasons of prosperity (sunshine), and seasons of adversity and hardship (rain, monsoons).

Is their purpose in our pain?

Our response to pain gives us an opportunity to align or realign our hearts with truth. Pain creates pressure, and pressure creates the possibility that we are more likely to go directly to our Father who is in Heaven. But, it's our response to pain, over time that changes us for the better or worse.

My Old Testament hero is David

I love this guy.

Why? David had an unusual focus on God during his teenage years.

David was 16 or 17 when he was anointed king of Israel—God's chosen people. David grew up to become a safe leader, the greatest military leader, the greatest poet, and the greatest songwriter in all of history.

David's writings let me know that it's okay to express my heart and complaint to God, without being struck dead. How does my Old Testament hero respond to pain? What does he do when despair consumes him? Lets see.

Psalm 59

The context of this Psalm is set in I Samuel 19. David was in his early 20's. Saul sent messengers to David's house with the intent to kill him. David began to cry out, "Deliver me from my enemies, O my God!"

David saw God as his source of comfort.

When we take our pain to God, we give Him an opportunity to change our entire perspective regarding the crises, adversity or situation.

See Different–Think Different–Respond Different–Feel Different.

When we see our adversity differently, we think about our situation differently. When we think differently, we respond differently, and over time, we feel different inside.

Venting to others may give us a moment of comfort. Our friends may offer us a Band-Aid* for our soul, and thank God for friends with Band-Aids*, but when we wake up tomorrow we're going to hurt again.

Connect with the big picture.

We don't want to lose an opportunity to be transformed by our painful experiences. And we desperately need our Heavenly Father's perspective. David continues in Psalm 59:3-16 telling God of his innocence!

"The political leaders of the nation are against me. I haven't been disloyal to Saul! Wake up God! Help me out here. Get involved— intervene on my behalf. Look God, these guys are like a pack of wild dogs, they're killer dogs, stop them! And, here's what I'm going to do—God I will sing of Your strength, I will joyfully sing of Your love and kindness in the morning, for you have been my stronghold and my refuge in the day of my distress." (Paraphrase added)

I don't know if this prayer or song was born in an hour, or over the course of months. But, I love it because David gives us insight on how to respond in our hour of crises.

King Saul continued to be David's chief enemy, and eventually, David became fearful.

What does David do when the crises escalate and the pressure increases?

The fear of man and the fear of death ensnared him. This led David to compromise. In his late twenties, David told a very big lie to Ahimelech, the priest. (I Sam. 21) David sought refuge among the Philistines, because he knew Saul was afraid of war with them. But, the Philistines recognized David as the one who killed Goliath. David became very afraid and faked madness to conceal himself. Then he escaped to the cave of Adullam.

In first Samuel 22, his brothers found out where he was hiding, and his father's household joined him. They came with some serious manpower—four hundred men.

I would agree that David could've used a little extra help right then! The only problem was, that every one of these men was in personal distress, steeped in financial problems, and very discontent about life.

David's response is like, "Okay, I'm going to use this pressure to drive me into Your heart."

Psalm 34

> I will bless the LORD at all times; His praise (the song of his heart to the LORD) shall continually be in my mouth... I sought the LORD, and He answered me, and delivered me from all my fears... This poor man (I was a fugitive, running for my life, I disobeyed the LORD, I lost all of my income, my family and friends) cried, and the LORD heard him and saved him out of all his troubles... Come, you children, listen to me; I will teach you the fear of the LORD (how to walk free from the fear of man)... The righteous cry, and the LORD hears and delivers them out of all their troubles. The LORD is near to the broken-hearted and saves those who are crushed in spirit (nearness to God is a reality for anyone who wants it, no matter how messed up or broken you think you are). Many are the afflictions of the righteous, but the LORD delivers him out of them all... (Parenthetical added)

Struggles don't define who you are.

Most of us define ourselves by our pain and our struggles; but God defines us by the *cry* in our heart. He defines us by what we long for. We define ourselves by what we no longer have, or by what or who we've lost.

I call them banners: "I'm rejected. I'm abandoned. I'm fatherless. I'm not loved. I'm a sinner. I'm a hypocrite. I'm a failure."

These are titles or banners that hang like a dark cloud above our heads based on our response to painful experiences. This is how we define ourselves. But, God *doesn't* define us by our achievements, successes or failures. He defines us by what we *long* for in our hearts.

David's Pressure Increases

Saul and his men came to Nob. Saul was paranoid that Ahimelech and David were partnered in a conspiracy against him. So, in a bloody massacre, he had his servant kill Ahimelech, 85 priests, plus women, children, and animals. (I Sam. 22:9-18)

God sent David and his men to deliver the city of Keilah. While David and his men were winning the war at Keilah, the Amalakites took their wives and children, and burned everything. David's men were ready to kill him.

David is crushed and in despair.

David was in utter despair. He caused the priests' murders, and his family was taken captive. His spirit was overwhelmed.

David must have thought:

The enemy has crushed my heart. I can't see anything. I'm in utter darkness. I can't feel God. I can't figure a way out of this one. The only thing that sustains me is that I know that You know, what I am going through.

Psalm 139:1-5

O LORD, You have searched me and known me. You know when I sit down and when I rise up; You understand my thought from afar. You scrutinize my path and my lying down, And are intimately acquainted with all my ways. Even before there is a word on my tongue, behold O LORD, You know it all.

David finds his comfort in the LORD.

David shows us that we must realign our hearts with TRUTH (which is reality). The Apostle Paul calls it the "renewing of our mind" in Romans 12:2.

Pain in and of itself isn't good. It's our response to pain that matters.

David constantly fed his soul truth. Most of the time, truth looked different than circumstances would indicate. Nevertheless, David was great at realigning his heart, mind, and soul with God's truth. This was David's model of transformation—speak the truth out loud. Even a faint whisper can make a difference. "Faith comes from *hearing*, and hearing by the WORD OF CHRIST." (Rom.10:17, emphasis added)

Disappearing for days and weeks into books, TV, movies, games, food, and other forms of entertainment, does not build our faith when we're in pain. Faith comes one way, by hearing the word of God.

Pressure and pain give us an opportunity to go back to the source, our Father, again and again. Let the pain of your life drive you all the way into His heart. He longs to be your source of comfort.

Chapter 14

Comforted By God

"Blessed are they that mourn, for they shall be comforted."
—Jesus, Matthew 5:4

People ask me all the time, "Cheryl, how did you survive so much trauma? How did you conquer your personal battle with depression, suicidal ideas, and a suicide attempt? And just when you overcame your struggle, you were faced with your father's suicide. How did you survive?"

And, while I'm so very grateful for the countless hours that beloved friends and skilled counselors listened to my heart, there is only one answer—God comforted me.

My precious friends, and caring counselors, *a necessary social support*, allowed me the opportunity to examine my war wounds in their presence. They'd sit with me through many nights and into the early morning, to make sure that my wounds weren't getting infected. But eventually, every conversation would end with them redirecting my broken heart to the God of all comfort.

Comforted by food.

I wasn't happy unless I had my favorite junk food combo. I can taste it now: a deep bite of chocolate and peanut butter from a Reese's cup, followed by the salty taste from Lay's all-natural classic potato chips, chased with a kick in your mouth that only a Dr. Pepper with twenty-three flavors can give you. Yes, this was certainly one of my favorite comfort food combos.

I would always tell myself, "If I can just get my combo fix, I'll be all right! I'll be able to make it through the day!"

On average, I think it took about fifteen minutes to consume this delicious combo. And it was a great fifteen minutes!

But, invariably I was guaranteed to need another delicious combo fix every two to three hours, which meant that every couple of months every part of my body would swell another inch.

Now, I know some of you are saying, "Oh, girl, if that was my only addiction, I'd be in really good shape." Trust me, I wasn't in good shape. I had other food addictions.

Fast Comfort Food! Philly Cheese Steak Hoagies on a soft Amoroso roll with fried onions, tomatoes, extra pickles and mayonnaise. And, I love Mexican food! Can you say Chipotle' chicken burritos with sour cream, guacamole, and mild salsa? And more Dr. Pepper's! Lord, have mercy! And how could I ever forget KFC's 2-piece breast and wing dinner combo, complete with mashed potatoes and gravy and a side of coleslaw, please!

Do you think my desperate need for comfort food stopped there? No! I was crazy about 7-Eleven's *Fresh To Go* brownie with a quart of creamy whole milk.

Well, what's a single Christian woman supposed to do? I had to anesthetize the pain of my broken heart!

Usually, within just a few short hours after consuming my favorite foods, I'd have a reality check. The pain of my heart would make its way through miles of junk food and fight to be at the top of the food chain. My profound need for comfort would become painfully clear. Now what?

Sometimes this would go on for months, till I was unable to zip up my blue jeans, and the pain of my heart threatened to sentence me to a lifetime of obesity and sorrow.

Then, in the height of my distress, I sent an SOS to the only one who could save me.

"Help me, God! Help! I desperately need You!
I'm drowning in despair, and the pain of my great loss!
I can't live like this, God!
I need You!
You're my only hope, You're my only salvation.
Rescue me. Save me. Please!"

Faint of heart, physically weak, and emotionally devastated, I fell to my knees, assumed a fetal-like position, and rocked back and forward, back and forward, on the floor, and simply whispered the name

"Jesus."
Gasping for air.
"Jesus!"
It felt like my heart would explode.
"Jesus."
I continued to whisper His name.

I needed one thing--to be comforted by God

But, would He hear my cry?
Could He hear my faint whisper?
Would He respond?

Psalm 18:1-19

The back-story for this passage is that Saul is consumed with anger, jealousy, suspicion, murder, and plots to kill David. In this hour of crises, David is hiding in the caves. David said,

> The cords of death encompassed me, And the torrents (floods) of ungodliness made me afraid. The cords of Sheol (the grave) surrounded about me; the snares of death confronted me. (Ps. 18:4-5, parenthetical added)

David was surrounded by men who wanted to kill him. He was trapped inside this cave. They'd set a snare for him! He was getting one death threat after another. He was overwhelmed, so he sent a distress signal. He sent an SOS call—Psalm 18:6:

In my distress I called upon the LORD, and cried to my God for help: He heard my voice out of his temple, and my cry before him came into his ears.

God hears your cry to Him for help.

Have you experienced stress lately?
What does it look like?
How do you typically handle stressful situations?

God's heart moves when He hears your cry.

David's enemies were God's enemies. God is passionate about injustice, and He's going to do something about it. "Then the earth shook and quaked; The foundations also of the mountains quaked and were shaken, because he was angry." (Ps. 18:7)

I love to see and feel the Lord's zeal. I love the descriptive imagery. Let's see how He responded to David's cry.

Psalm 18:8a, "Smoke went up out of his nostrils..."

Have you ever been so angry that it felt like smoke was coming out of your nose?

And fire from his mouth devoured: Coals were kindled by it. He bowed the heavens also, and came down... And he rode upon a cherub, and flew; Yea, he soared upon the wings of the wind. He made darkness his hiding-place... The LORD also thundered in the heavens, and the Most High uttered his voice, Hailstones and coals of fire. And he sent out His arrows, and scattered them; Yea, lightning's flashed in abundance, and routed them... At Your rebuke, O LORD, At the blast of the breath of Your nostrils. (Ps. 18:8b-15)

Look how God responds to David's cry! Can you see the lightening and hear the thunder? Can you picture the hailstones and coals of fire coming down out of the sky? This is the zeal and the passion of the Lord when He hears a distress call from the one that He loves.

Psalm 18:16

"He sent from on high, He took me; He drew me out of many waters."

Oh, I love this.

Did you know that God is a compassionate, certified, rescue swimmer with the Coast Guard?

The phrase, "many waters" simply means many life-threatening problems.

Do you ever feel like you are in life-threatening waters and/or situations?

Are the waters so deep, the waves so big, the currents so strong, that you feel like you could possibly drown?

Psalm 18:17

"He delivered me from my strong enemy, And from them that hated me; for they were too mighty for me."

God delivers us from our strongest enemies, from those who hate us, and from situations that are too overwhelming for us.

Psalm 18:18

"They confronted me in the day of my calamity; But the LORD was my stay."

God will be your stay, your anchor and your support in the hour of crises.

Psalm 18:19

"He brought me forth also into a large (broad) place..." (Parenthetical added)

God will take what the enemy meant for evil and will use it for our good.

Remember Joseph?

His brothers sold him into slavery.

He went to prison, then to Potiphar's house; back to prison, then, made ruler of Egypt.

Joseph was given the king's signet ring, clothing and accessories. He was riding large and folks in the street were bowing when he passed.

He received supernatural wisdom to store food for a famine. When it came, he opened the storehouses. People traveled far to eat at Joe's! (Gen. 39)

Once delivered, once you overcome your temporary personal crisis, you will come into a large, broad place. Your sphere of influence will change. You'll get double for *all* of your trouble.

You might be in the pit now, but when you emerge, you may find many people approaching you as an expert, a deliverer to lead them to the Mighty Deliverer.

Remember Moses?

He had a death sentence and was placed in a watery grave in an attempt to save his life. He was found and brought into the kingdom of Egypt's lavish settings, which included an Ivy League education. He said goodbye to all of it, and searched for his Hebrew family. He was raised up as a powerful deliverer who led God's people to freedom. (Ex. 12–15)

And, let's not forget Esther.

She becomes an orphan. Her uncle Mordecai, a Jewish exile, takes care of Esther. She's taken to the king's palace and made queen with a royal crown placed on her head (broad, large place). Esther saves the king's life by exposing an evil plot to annihilate all of the

Jews, her people and God's chosen people—and becomes a deliverer. (Est. 5–8)

Here comes my favorite part of the story.

Psalm 18:19

"He rescued me, because He delighted in me."

What? I've been rescued because God *likes* me and *enjoys* me! Yes, Yes, Yes.

Even in my weakest moments, even while I'm in the process of maturing, God likes me! He enjoys me!

This truth gives us confidence to run to God in our weakest, most desperate moments. We can boldly, with God-confidence, approach the throne of grace and receive mercy.

He's the God of all comfort

The only way to find comfort is to realign your heart with this truth. You can't change your emotions; but you can renew your mind, change your thoughts, and over time, God will change your emotions. It takes time, be patient, it will happen.

When your heart has revelation, your emotions feel it!

I remember another time when I desperately needed to be comforted by God.

For SIX months during my prayer time, I was in deep anguish over my sin, my weaknesses and my failures.

I would groan in agony.

Why?

Because the things I desperately did not want to do were the very things I found myself doing. And, the things I sincerely wanted to do, I felt powerless to accomplish.

I felt like a hopeless hypocrite.

I feared that God was weary of my coming to Him again and again with the same issues.

I hated my sin.

I despised my weaknesses.

I mourned my failures.

I cried, "Abba, let me hate the things that you hate and love the things that you love."

Despite my prayers of repentance and pleas for help, little seemed to change. Until the night the Lord encountered me in a dream.

Here's The Dream...

Suddenly, I was standing eye-to-eye with a man.

No words were spoken between us.

I looked deeply into his eyes, and knew everything about him.

I saw that he was a good man, but he did not have a personal relationship with the Lord.

Then, the Lord whispered in my ear, "Now, I'm going to let you *feel* My love for this man."

Immediately, I felt the tangible, manifest presence of God's unconditional love and HIS heart for this man.

It was powerful!

It was the kind of feeling you never want to end.

Then, the Lord whispered, "Now, I'm going to let you *feel* his love back for Me."

Right away, I felt this man's love for God. His heart was cold toward God.

All of a sudden, that man disappeared and a second man stood eye-to-eye with me.

Not one word was spoken between us.

I looked intently in his eyes and knew everything about him.

He'd been a believer from his childhood. And for most of his life He walked in the ways of the Lord.

The Lord whispered in my ear, "Now, I'm going to let you *feel* My love for this man."

Instantly, I felt the tangible, manifest presence of God's unconditional love and heart for this man.

It's the kind of feeling you never want to end.

God's love did not change at all from the first man to the second man.

That's interesting! I thought.

The Lord said, "Now, I'm going to let you *feel* his love back for Me."

Right away, I could feel this man's love and tender heart for God.

Swiftly, he disappeared and a third man stood eye-to-eye with me.

No words were spoken.

I looked steadily in his eyes and knew he'd known the Lord for about 25% of his life.

The Lord said, "Now, I'm going to let you *feel* My love for this man."

Without delay, I felt the tangible, manifest presence of God's love and heart for this man.

It's the kind of feeling that you never want to end.

I was stunned!

God's love did not change from the first man, to the second, or to the third.

By this point, I was completely fascinated.

His love remained consistent, unchanged and equally powerful.

The Lord said, "Now, I'm going to let you *feel* his love back for me."

This man's love for God was distinctly stronger than the second man.

I was astonished.

In a flash, that man disappeared and a fourth man stood in front of me.

But, this man did not stand eye-to-eye with me.

Instead, he stood with his back to me.

A movie screen of his life played before my eyes.

He was a Believer.

He loved the Lord.

Yet, I could see him failing miserably in the present.

I could see him struggling with his sin.

I identified with this man's struggle.

But, in my heart I thought.

There's no way the Lord's love for this guy is going to be the same as the first, second or the third man. It's impossible. Look at this guy—he's too ashamed to look me in the eye.

This man looked heavenward over his right shoulder.

In the weakest of voice, I watched him cry out to God for help.

His countenance was filled with desperation and anguish.

I could feel the ache, and grief in his heart over his sin.

The Lord said, "Now, I'm going to let you *feel* My love for this man."

Surely, God's love for him would be significantly less, I thought.

Immediately, the Lord allowed me to feel His unconditional love and heart for this man.

I was shocked!

It was the same tangible manifest presence of God's unconditional love.

It's the kind of feeling that you never want to end.

Inside, I screamed.

How is that possible? Do You see what I see? I don't understand.

Then, the Lord tenderly whispered in my ear.

"Now, I'm going to let you feel what I **get to feel**."

It was as if God was going to share one of His greatest pleasures with me, and He did!

What I felt next rocked my world.

This man's love for the Lord was off the charts, friend, off the charts!

It was passionate, wholehearted love with wild abandon.

It was red hot, fiery love. It was so intense it took my breath away.

Gasping for air I cried, "How can this be?"

With delight the Lord whispered.

"He who's been forgiven much loves much."

The dream ended.

I was suddenly awake.

I felt the tangible presence of God resting on me.

My heart was filled with awe and wonder at the heart of God.

I could still hear His words ringing in my ear.

"I'm going to let you feel what I **get to** *feel...***get to** *feel...***get to** *feel.*"

It had been so long since I'd felt His nearness—I did not want to move.

What was it about this last man that moved Your heart so deeply? I asked.

The Lord responded.

"Did you see his face?"

"Yes, he gave You a slight glance."

"Yes, but it was a sincere glance. Did you hear his cry?"

"Yes, I heard his weak cry," I said.

"Oh, but it was a genuine cry that *moved* My heart with compassion, love and mercy," He said.

"Even the slightest glance My way, even the weakest cry to Me for help, even in his weakness, even in his immaturity, he is a lover of God. He hates what I hate. And he loves what I love. He pursues righteousness. He aggressively wars against the lust of his flesh. Therefore, his love is real, and authentic, and it *moves* My heart."

That night, my Father came and set my heart free from a self-imposed prison sentence. God comforted my heart.

Have you ever experienced a time when God comforted you? If so, what happened?

Maybe you're saying, "Cheryl, I'm glad you had that experience, but I'm not sure that God has the comfort that I need." Allow me to share a few more passages about this God of ALL comfort with you.

A Divine Exchange

Isaiah 61:1-3 gives us more insight about the God of comfort:

The Spirit of the Lord God is on me because the LORD has anointed me to bring *good news* to the afflicted; He has sent me to bind up the brokenhearted, to proclaim *liberty* to captives and *freedom* to prisoners; to proclaim the favorable year of the LORD and the day of vengeance of our God;

to comfort all who mourn, to grant those who mourn in Zion, giving them a garland instead of ashes, the oil of gladness instead of mourning, the mantle of praise instead of a spirit of fainting. So they will be called oaks of righteousness, the planting of the LORD that He may be glorified. (emphasis added)

Are you afflicted in body, mind or soul?
Are you brokenhearted?
Are you held captive to something or someone?
Are you in prison?
Are you mourning a loss?

If you answered yes to one or several questions, I assure you that God offers you comfort, today.

He wants to make a divine exchange with you, right now.

He offers comfort to the afflicted, the brokenhearted, the captive, the prisoner, and those who grieve.

God wants to offer you freedom, liberty, justice, gladness, a song in your heart and comfort.

How about it?

Are you ready to make that exchange?

Paul reminds us in II Corinthians 1:3-6:

"Blessed be the God and Father of our Lord Jesus Christ, the Father of mercies and God of all comfort, who comforts us in all our affliction so that we will be able to comfort those who are in any affliction with the comfort with which we ourselves are comforted by God. For just as the sufferings of Christ are ours in abundance, so also our comfort is abundant through Christ."

Paul tells us the sufferings of Christ are ours in abundance, but also our comfort is abundant through Christ.

The good news is that God comforts us in ALL our affliction.

Paul continues:

"For we do not want you to be unaware, brethren, of our affliction which came to us in Asia, that we were burdened excessively, beyond our strength, so that we despaired even of life; indeed, we had the sentence of death within ourselves so that we would not trust in ourselves, but in God who raises the dead; who delivered us from so great a peril of death, and will deliver us He on whom we have set our hope. And He will yet deliver us…" (II Cor. 1:8–10)

"Beloved," Paul says, "Yes, we were burdened excessively, beyond our strength, so that we despaired even of life itself."

He goes on to say, "But, I know this about God, He raises the dead, and He delivers us from perils of death, and He will YET deliver us…"

What are your afflictions?

Are you burdened excessively?

Is your burden beyond your strength physically and/or emotionally?

Have you recently despaired of your own life?

I have good news for you.
Set your hope in God.
He will YET deliver you.

You say, "Cheryl, I'm depressed." Beloved, I have more good news for you. Paul reminds us in II Corinthians 7:6 that "God, who comforts the depressed comforted us…"

God comforts the depressed.

I suffered with acute depression for nearly a decade.

I suffered with an affective disorder.

I had many depressive episodes.

But, when I truly allowed my Father to comfort me in all my afflictions, when I received His comfort for my broken heart, when I accepted His promise to make all the wrong things right, in His time, I received freedom, liberty, justice, gladness and a song in my heart.

Beloved, it was the best exchange I'd ever made.

If you're depressed, I want to encourage you to cry out to the LORD in your distress. I understand that you may feel you haven't the strength to say your own name, right now. It's okay. Simply look in His direction and whisper His name. God, too, can comfort you.

Chapter 15

A Living Hope

"The future is worth expecting."
–Henry David Thoreau

Hope has been a very special word for me since I was a teenager. I have long loved the word *Hope.*

Years ago, I named my car Hope. And, though it's just a simple one-syllable word, I love the way it sounds. I love the way it makes my heart feel.

If I ever have the opportunity to give birth to a little girl I most assuredly will name her Hope. If you are pregnant with a little girl, I suggest the name Hope for your lovely daughter, too. In fact, name your cat, your bird or your little hamster, Hope.

I think you understand.

I love the word/name Hope.

But why?

I'm so glad you asked.

When I was 13 years old, I was in front of the television late one evening, at my grandma's house. I watched one of those 80's action/ police dramas. If my memory serves me correctly, it may have been *HUNTER.* Rick Hunter was a homicide detective who along with his female partner, Dee Dee McCall, would investigate Los Angeles' most bizarre murders. This particular episode was a murder-suicide story.

During the show, I saw hopeless, despairing young people who'd concluded that their lives no longer mattered.

They lived without purpose.

They lived without hope.

They were angry about the circumstances life had dealt them. And they sought revenge.

The storyline continued to investigate the murder/suicide.

This is someone's reality, I thought. *This really happens every day, somewhere.*

Suddenly, an arrow from Heaven pierced my heart. I began to sob and sob; my heart was marked by God. I heard Him call me to bring a message of hope to those who were so hopeless that they desired to end their lives by suicide.

At 13, the message of hope and Jesus were synonymous to me. I thought all I'd need to do, is to tell someone about Jesus and they'd be transformed from hopeless to hope-filled. This is what I expected to happen. *After all,* I reasoned, *this is what hope, as a verb, means. It means to expect, to trust, to anticipate, to wish or to look forward to. And, well, that was my hope.*

I used to think hope was about being positive. I thought, *Jesus is positive, Heaven is positive, and that's the hope I'm called to bring to the hopeless. I hope it works!*

And then life happened.

In my early 20's, I started to realize that hope, as a verb, was not sturdy enough for me.

I submitted a vacation request form to my employer once, and hoped they'd approve the specific dates for my trip, already planned and paid for. But what if they didn't? My hope was shaky, not certain, not guaranteed. I didn't like that feeling.

I remember a time when I left home without allowing enough time to catch my flight. On my way to the airport, I was full of hope the airline would excuse my tardiness, and let me board. But when I arrived, the agent said, "I'm sorry. You've already missed your flight. You'll need to wait here, on standby, for another one."

The news was quite disappointing to me.

Did *hope* disappoint me?

I mean I was full of expectation that I wouldn't miss my flight. But in the end, I missed the flight. I was too late.

I'd lost confidence in *hope* as a verb.

Soon, I began to say,

"There's gotta be something more to this *hope* thing. Because as of late, hope has disappointed me too many times."

I need hope that goes beyond me.

I need hope that has power beyond the sting of someone's negative or evil words spoken to me or about me.

I need hope that goes beyond my own reaching for personal success.

I need hope that can weather the turbulence of my life.

I need hope that offers me security beyond my 401K or savings account.

I need hope that offers me stability beyond graduation.

To get a job.

To have a career.

To get married.

To have kids.

To watch them grow up.

To send them off to college.

To graduate.

So they can have a career

and get married

and have their own house, kids, and husband or wife

and retire

and like the soap opera, *Days Of Our Lives* says,

"Like sand through the hourglass, these are the days of our lives."

And, on and on it goes and goes.

But where?

I needed hope to be anchored to something.

I needed to have confidence in God's promises related to my future. I needed to be able to trust hope. I needed more than a mere concept of hope. I needed something that was certain and sure.

Many times we're counseled by friends and loved ones, to look inward, to look at social, and environmental circumstances, to look at our past—to understand our present. And this is necessary.

But, rarely does anyone tell us to *look forward*. Yet, this is a critical part of our emotional health. We must look forward if we're going to have the right perspective that will transform our heart and emotions.

We lose hope when we don't understand the dream in God's heart for us, our eternal destiny and inheritance—that awaits us. We lose heart and motivation to make good choices, to overcome life's challenges and our failures, and to resist temptation and yield to every craving our flesh desires. Then it becomes so much easier to give in to rejection, hopelessness and despair.

A Living Hope--I Peter 1:3-9:

> Blessed be the God and Father of our LORD Jesus Christ, who...has caused us to be born again to a LIVING HOPE... to obtain an inheritance which is imperishable and undefiled and will not fade away reserved in heaven for you...In this you GREATLY REJOICE, even though now for a little while...you have been distressed by various trials...Prepare your minds for action, keep sober in spirit, and fix your HOPE completely on the grace to be brought to you at the revealing of Jesus Christ. (emphasis added)

Peter, that was a gigantic mouthful of revelation. Let's look at this passage a little closer. First understand we've been born to a LIVING HOPE!

Friend, this is good news.

HOPE LIVES!

Hope isn't dead.

It's living, breathing, and active.

This living hope carries the power to dynamically impact our mind, our thoughts, and our emotions.

This living HOPE is connected to a future event—the revealing of Jesus, at His second coming.

This living hope holds the promise that when Jesus returns, we have an inheritance waiting for us, and nobody can tamper with it. It can never be taken away from us or be corrupted.

Wait a minute, Peter. Did you just say that I have an inheritance? Really! What kind of inheritance?

Well, what is it? And, where is it?

"Reserved in Heaven for you..." (I Peter 1:4)

Do you think about Heaven?
>**How often do you think about Heaven?**
>>**What do you think Heaven is going to be like?**

So, Peter, uh, these fiery trials, they're on purpose?
You and James are starting to sound a lot alike.

James 1:2-6:

Consider it all joy, my brethren, when you encounter various trials, knowing (having confidence, hope) that the testing of your faith produces endurance (now). And, let endurance have its perfect (maturing) result, so that you may be perfect (mature) and complete, lacking in nothing (on the day you stand one-on-one with Jesus at the Judgment seat—when you get your inheritance). But if any of you lacks wisdom (about the various fiery trials), let him ask of God, who gives to all generously and without reproach, and it will be given to him. (Parenthetical added)

Now, James, did you just ask me to consider all of my fiery trials as *joy*? And, did you connect my fiery trials today to another day, the day I stand before Jesus at the Judgment seat, the place of rewards?

Let me make sure I understand you, James.

So, everything I'm going through right now is actually giving me an opportunity to persevere, to endure, and to help me mature because God wants me to get my full inheritance?

Wow!

Cool.

He did say, "If we suffer with Him we would also reign (rule, govern) with Him," (II Tim. 2:12, parenthetical added).

Thanks, James!

I hadn't considered that before.

I just thought everybody, including the Devil, was out to get me, you know. Now, I'm going to approach these fiery trials differently, with perspective—eternal perspective.

Thanks again, James!

Oh yeah, but, what's my inheritance?

Okay, here's a clue.

It's not just that Jesus returns; its what happens after He returns. Jesus is coming, yes, but He's coming to restore all things.

(Acts 3:19)

Have you ever felt that you were made for more than you are, more than you've become, more than others have given you an opportunity to be?

Have you ever said, "There must be more than this?"

If so, you're right.

There is so much more than this.

That's the good news!

It's connected to eternity, and the ultimate dream in God's heart for you.

Do you know the dream in God's heart for you?

Perhaps, you're saying, "Cheryl, I hope to God it's a bigger dream than the life I'm living. I hope this isn't all there is to life."

I have good news for you, my friend.

The dream in God's heart for you is *bigger* than any dream you've ever imagined for yourself.

In Heaven everything is PERFECT.

Want a glimpse of Your new home?
Read Revelation 21-22:1-5
The New Jerusalem—the 1,500-mile Crystal City.
Think about the city's design.
Its length, width, and height are equal.
Think of the dimensions of this design.
In 2010, the tallest building in the world is in Dubai.
The building is 2,716 feet tall—one hundred sixty stories.
Now imagine a city that is 1,500 miles high.
How many stories might that be?
And the Crystal City is pure gold—like crystal clear jewels.

The illuminated city.

God Himself is there.
Light emanates from His being.
His being emanates indescribable kindness, love, and mercy.
He's transparent.
There's no darkness in Him.
We'll see Him face to face.
The glorious light of God surrounds us and fills us, and lights up the entire city.

Can you imagine how brilliant and dazzling this city is?

The foundation stones of this city are precious stones:
Jasper; Sapphire; Chalcedony; Emerald; Sardonyx; Sardius; Chrisolite; Beryl; Topaz; Chrysoprase; Jacinth and Amethyst.
Oh, the colors in this city. They're more vibrant than anything we are familiar with on earth. But, try to imagine.
Our botanical gardens will pale in comparison to the vivacious colors of the trees, fields, and flowers.

Oh, the splendor and majesty of this city.

The city has twelve gates, which are twelve pearls—each gate is a single pearl—imagine.

The 24-hour gated community guarded by Angels is never closed.

Yet, nothing unclean, wicked or evil can enter into this city.

The streets of the city are pure gold—like transparent glass.

There's no night.

This celestial city far exceeds all the opulence, beauty or luxury you could ever imagine.

The most luxurious elite five-star Hotel will look like a dilapidated shanty next to your eternal living quarters.

Come to the most lavish banquet for the whole family.

You will enjoy the finest food and experience the most amazing flavor combinations that will confirm one thing.

You are indeed in Heaven.

You will drink the purest water and taste refined aged wine and enjoy amazing fellowship with old friends and new, and loved ones too. (Isaiah 25:6)

The joyous celebration never ceases.

The happy hour never ends.

You will feel more love than you've ever known in your life.

The love of God will fill and surround you.

All your worries will be gone FOREVER. No more anxiety.

You will experience unimaginable joy, peace, happiness and love.

Hear. See. Taste. Smell. Touch.

Our five senses, dull on the earth, will be fully alive here.

The atmosphere of Heaven is filled with glorious music and songs—as people from every tongue, tribe and nation sing with myriads of angels—unending melodies of praise:

"Great and marvelous are Your works, O Lord God, the Almighty; Righteous and true are Your ways, King of the nations! (Rev. 15:3)

The worshipping city.

There will be no more *Somebody Did Somebody Wrong* songs.

Only songs of joyful worship and adoration, to our God and King, will be heard and sung in this city.

Imagine the notes, the tones, and the melodies of Heaven.

Imagine the harmonies of Heaven!

Its music fills you with unspeakable joy, peace, hope, faith and love. Oh, the fragrance of worship and adoration.

You're part of the music and the music is part of you.

If you were tone deaf, or pitch challenged on earth—guess what?   Your pitch will be PERFECT and you'll join the heavenly choir and sing:

"Hallelujah! Salvation, and glory and power belong to our God; Because His Judgments are true and righteous." (Rev. 19:1-2).

In other words, "God, You led my life in perfection. Your judgments weren't too harsh—they were right."

Angels of harmony sing with resurrected human beings.

What will the choirs sound like?

I imagine the calm of many waters, but the strength and power of thunder.

This is your home—forever.

Magnificent Body Makeover.

Think about it!

You're going to get a brand new physical body that looks just like yours—only it will be perfect.

You won't have excess body weight.

The wrinkles and fine lines will all be gone.

You won't have acne scars.

You won't be bald.

You won't have to wear dentures.

You won't have to wear any prosthetic limbs.

You won't need your walking stick or walker.

You won't need your eyeglasses or contacts.

Your body will have supernatural qualities (Philippians 3:20-21).

You will be able to walk thru walls.

Imagine being able to teleport from one side of the celestial city to the other instantaneously.

And, the river of life—imagine swimming in it.

What will the crystal clear water be like?

Will it have musical qualities to it?

What will the 12 kinds of fruit be like from the tree of life?

And the leaves of this amazing tree are for the healing of the nations.

This will be your home—forever.

You won't ever be evicted. And did you know that the dream in God's heart has always been—to live with you in the paradise of Heaven and on the EARTH, together in eternal bliss, face-to-face, forever and ever, with both the natural realm and the supernatural realm, united together in one, as it was in the beginning? (Rev. 21:2-3,10; Gen.1-2).

Ephesians 1:9-10 tells us "He made known the mystery of His will (the hidden plan)...that He might gather together *in one ALL* things, in Christ both which are in heaven and which are on earth." (parenthetical and emphasis added)

We will administrate His government with Him.

His bond-servants will serve Him and reign with Him forever and ever. Kings and priests to our God...we shall reign on the earth. (Rev. 5:10)

Priests worship, intercede, and communicate the knowledge of God. Kings have judicial responsibility and authority: to evaluate, create action plans, appoint people into different spheres of society to train, manage and govern restoration projects and assignments.

"Well done good and faithful servant...I will make you ruler over many things." (Matthew 25:23)

You will take pleasure in your work on earth as you work with Jesus, during the thousand-year reign to restore the cities and nations of earth, and every sphere of society:

Arts/Entertainment
Business (Is. 60)
Education
Family (Is. 66:22)
Government (Is. 9:6-7; Is. 11)
Agricultural (Is. 35)
Environment (Is. 65:17)

Everything will be progressively restored to the Garden of Eden reality using supernaturally enhanced natural processes.

(Acts 3:20-21; Is. 51:3; Is. 11)

Cities and nations will be rebuilt and restored. (Isaiah 61:4-6)

Imagine a day when we will have ONLY righteous leaders, rulers and judges on the earth.

It will be a physical, material world united with the supernatural, heavenly world, and we will live together forever in God's presence, with the Lamb, Jesus, and with the angels.

He will make all the wrong things right.

There will be no more shame.
No more sickness.
No more pain.
No more grief.
No more death.
The heavens and the earth will be fully restored—made new.
No more tears
And no more sorrow.

"God will wipe away every tear from their eyes; there shall be no more death, nor sorrow, nor crying. There will be no more pain, for the former things have passed away." (Rev. 21:4)

Can you imagine? This is your future. It's PAIN FREE!

This is your inheritance, my friend! This is the living hope!

Your life isn't mostly about your 70 plus years here.

This life is mostly to grow in love, in meekness, in humility, and in servanthood, in preparation for the next billion years.

Your destiny is BEYOND anything you could ever imagine and it's connected to ETERNITY.

This hope is living and is anchored in Heaven.

It's not a fairy tale.

If you know Jesus, this is your story.

This gives perspective to your daily struggles and pain.

There's something bigger going on.

Paul gives us a key to how we should carry our hearts in times of adversity, persecution, loss of health or family crises:

Keep seeking the things above, where Christ is...
set your mind on things above, not on the things
that are on the (unrestored) earth.
(Col. 3:1-2, parenthetical added)

Hope is a clear picture of a future that is promised us.

Hope changes the way we think.

Hope gives us motivation to make right choices, to have a good work ethic, and to give us perspective on how we process loneliness and rejection.

Hope strengthens us with supernatural resolve to endure and overcome life's circumstances.

Hope must be an anchor in our present life.

How do we do this?

1. Talk about Heaven with others.
2. Meditate on the scriptures about the New Jersualem, the New Heavens, and the New Earth (referenced in this chapter).
3. Ask the Holy Spirit to give you wisdom and revelation about your eternal destiny and inheritance.
4. Read stories about Heaven and people who went there and returned. (See recommended reading list)

So, what's your story?

Everyone's journey is unique, and life's circumstances are varied yet, inside the heart of every human being, there is a cry for justice—a cry for wrong things to be made right.

While your story is probably very different from mine, life's injustices—real or perceived—are innumerable. Maybe it's betrayal, separation, divorce, the death of a loved one, the pressures of school, peer pressure, bullying, parental abuse/neglect, mid-life crisis, aging, chronic sickness, disease, pain, depression, mental illness, spousal abuse, economic pressure, political pressure, a terminal illness or a run in with the law. It could be emotional pain or trauma resulting from an accident or from an act of violence or from false allegations. Perhaps it's the loss of a job, a career, a 401K, a house, a car or a good name. The list of injustices goes on and on.

Suicide happens when one feels incapable of resolving a real or perceived injustice—when one feels powerless to make the wrong things right, and believes the only way to end their pain, is to end their life.

I want to remind you that the strength of my life and yours is Love's commitment to us. There is always *help*. There is always *hope*. We only need to find the courage to ask for it. You may not have it within yourself, but someone else can help you or refer you to someone who is capable of helping you through your crises.

It's been more than ten years since I've struggled with acute depression and suicidal ideas. Is it because I've managed to escape hardships or problems for ten years?

Absolutely *not*!

I still have my share of problems, challenges and hardships.

So, what's the difference?

I ask for help. I ask for perspective. I seek counsel. I realign my heart with *truth* (reality). And I believe that *Love* will never fail me. His *Stubborn Love* rescued me so many times and convinced me of His unfailing love and commitment. He convinced me that one day He would make all the wrong things in my life—right, and gave me the confidence to let go of all the injustices I had harbored within—crippling me.

Beloved, I close with Paul's prayer from Ephesians 3:14-20:

I bow my knees before my Father—from whom every family in heaven and on earth derives its name—that He would grant you, according to the riches of His glory, to be strengthened with power through His Spirit in your inner man, so that Christ may dwell in your hearts through faith; and that you, being rooted and grounded in love, may be able to comprehend with all the saints what is the breadth and length and height and depth, and to know (experientially) the love of Christ which surpasses all knowledge, that you may be filled up to all the fullness of God. Now to Him who is able to do far more abundantly beyond all that we ask or think, according to the power that works within us, to Him be the glory...forever and ever. Amen. (parenthetical added)

Beloved, His *Stubborn Love* will never let go of you—so never let go of Him! Never stop believing that one day He will make all the wrong things in your life right. Love never fails! Love will fight on your behalf. Give Love a chance! Give Him an opportunity to prove Himself to you.

Beloved, my prayer is that your inner man, your soul, your mind, will, and emotions will be anchored in His *Stubborn Love*, and you will make a recommitment to live—to choose *life*—and say yes to Love today!

6 Biggest and Deadliest Suicide Myths

Myth #1 – No one can stop suicide, it is inevitable.

Myth #2 – Confronting a person about suicide will only make a person angry and increase the risk of suicide.

Myth #3 – Only experts can prevent suicide.

Myth #4 – Suicidal people keep their plans to themselves.

Myth #5 – Once a person decides to complete suicide there is nothing anyone can do to stop them.

Myth #6 – Those who talk about suicide don't do it.

BECAUSE THE TRUTH IS...

Truth #1 – If people in a crisis get the help they need they will probably never be suicidal again.

Truth #2 – Asking someone about suicide intent lowers the anxiety, opens up communication, and lowers the risk of an impulsive act.

Truth #3 – Suicide prevention is everybody's business and everybody can help prevent the tragedy of suicide

Truth #4 – Most suicidal people communicate their intent sometime during the week preceding their attempt.

Truth #5 –Those who talk about suicide may try, or even complete an act of self- destruction.

Truth #6 – Suicide is the most preventable kind of death and almost any positive action can save a life.

Revised and used with permission by QPR Institute—QPR Myth and Facts

A Safety Agreement
A No-Suicide Contract

I,_____ promise that I will never attempt to kill myself accidentally, or on-purpose. I promise that I will not drink alcohol or use drugs. Instead, I will ask for help from a friend or a professional.

I promise that if I feel like I want to die by suicide, I will immediately call my family/friend _____, or _____, at the following phone numbers:

    1.) _____

    2.) _____

I WILL ASK FOR HELP

If for some reason, I am unable to reach either one by phone, I promise to call, **1-800-SUICIDE** immediately.

This Safety Agreement becomes effective today.

(Signed) _____

(Date) _____

Tear the Safety Agreement out of the book and post it where you can see it.

Resources

If you, or someone you know, is in emotional distress or suicidal crisis please call a free 24-hour hotline:

1-800-273-TALK or 1-800-SUICIDE

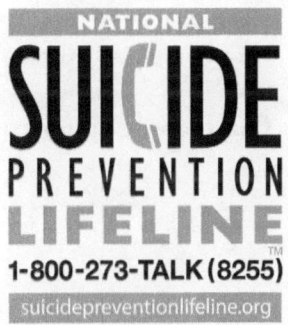

Your call will be routed to the nearest crisis center.
- **Call for yourself or someone you care about.**
- **Free and confidential.**
- **A network of more than 140 crisis centers nationwide.**

To reach a teen peer counselor, please call 877-YOUTHLINE, (877-968-8454)

Additional Online Resources

1. American Foundation For Suicide Prevention--www.afsp.org
2. Kristin Brooks Hope Center--www.hopeline.com
3. American Association of Suicidology--www.suicidology.org
4. Suicide Awareness Voices of Education--www.save.org
5. National Suicide Prevention Hotline--www.suicide preventionlifeline.org
6. Centre For Suicide Prevention--www.suicideinfo.ca
7. Suicide Prevention Resource Center--www.sprc.org

If you or someone you know is in emotional distress or suicidal crisis,

call

1-800-273-TALK (8255).
National Suicide Prevention Lifeline

Call today. Call now!

Recommended Reading

Download Dr. Paul Quinnett's free e-book, Suicide the Forever Decision. www.qprinstitute.com/Forever_Decision.zip

Dr. Quinnett wrote the book to a highly suicidal patient named "Mary" but intended it to be read by anyone thinking about suicide. It is a unique book in that it is written in the second person, as if the doctor and a patient are having a therapy session about suicide and its implications, not only for the suicidal person, but those who know, love and care for him or her.

Further Reading

Alcorn, Randy. 2004. *Heaven*. Carol Stream, IL. Tyndale House.

Anderson, Neil T. 2006. *The Bondage Breaker: Overcoming *Negative*

Thoughts *Irrational Feelings *Habitual Sins. Eugene, OR. Harvest House Publishers.

Anderson, Neil T. 2000. *Victory Over the Darkness: Realizing the Power of Your Identity in Christ*. Ventura, CA. Regal.

Billheimer, Paul E. 2006. Don't Waste Your Sorrows: Finding God's Purpose in the Midst of Pain. Bloomington, MN. Bethany House.

Burpo, Todd. 2010. Heaven is for Real: A Little Boys Astonishing Story of His Trip to Heaven and Back. Nashville, TN. Thomas Nelson.

Cobain, Bev. 1998. *When Nothing Matters Anymore: A Survival Guide for Depressed Teens.* Minneapolis: Free Spirit Publishing.

Hsu, Albert Y. 2002. *Grieving A Suicide: A Loved One's Search For Comfort, Answers & Hope.* Chicago, IL. InterVarsity Press.

Jamison, Kay Redfield. 1999. *Night Falls Fast: Understanding Suicide.* New York: Alfred A. Knopf. Repr. New York: Vintage Books, 2000.

Joiner, Thomas. 2005. *Why People Die by Suicide.* Cambridge, MA: Harvard University Press.

Macgirvin, Jackie. 2011. *Angels of Humility* (A novel). Shippensburg, PA: Destiny Image.

Quinnett, Paul. 1992. *Suicide: The Forever Decision—For Those Thinking About Suicide, and For Those Who Know, Love, or Counsel Them.* Revised edition. New York: Crossroad Publishing.